MONEY HELPS

FAMILIES

FAMILY FINANCIAL DISTRESS AND CHILD WELFARE

L. Anthony Loman PhD

Money Helps Families

Family Financial Distress and Child Welfare

L. Anthony Loman PhD

Kravitz & Sons
INNOVATORS IN PUBLISHING, MARKETING AND ADVERTISING

Kravitz and Sons LLC
204 E Arlington Blvd. Suite B
Greenville, NC 27858

Published by Kravitz and Sons LLC.

ISBN: 979-8-89639-905-6 (sc)
ISBN: 979-8-89639-904-9 (e)
ISBN: 979-8-89639-906-3 (hc)

Library of Congress Control Number: 2026909171

Table of Contents

Introduction

As the book title indicates, this is a book about financial problems in families. It is a subject that I and my colleagues have studied and researched for many years. I reference many of those studies and summarize a few in the following chapters. However, my interests are broader. How can the welfare of families, and in particular those with children, be improved?

The focus of the book is on American families but many of the findings and conclusions can be applied worldwide. We need to move toward more inclusive and less biased systems of support that permits human beings to develop and live their lives in relative good health and contentment.

In the first two chapters, economic hardships of families and their effects are examined. I consider the notions of child abuse and child neglect in Chapter 3, because that is one of the areas that I researched extensively. This is followed by a fourth chapter that outlines six extensive field studies of thousands of families in which financial supports were provided to families that were experiencing hardships. The long-term positive effects on the families and their children are shown

Then the book turns to more general causes, their contexts, and possible solutions in Chapter 5 through 8.

I hope you find the book informative and useful.

Chapter 1

Economic Hardship Among Families with Children

A. Does Poverty Really Exist in the United States?

At the extreme end of families in dire financial conditions are families in poverty. Poor children are those living in poor families. How many children live in families classified as poor? Looking at official statistics, there were 10,350,000 children (persons under 18 years old) living in poverty in the United States in 2024. This was 14.3% of all children—1 child out of every 7. Of those in poverty, 4,271,000 children were living in families with incomes at less than half the official poverty level.[1] In that year the poverty level for a family of four was $31,200 per year. Half that would be $15,600 or about $1,300 per month. This is extreme poverty. That over 10 million U.S. children live in deprived households and over 4 million in extremely deprived ones are startling numbers, given that the US is the richest country in the world, indeed in the history of the world. Yet, the US has very high levels of child poverty in comparison to other countries. In 2021 listings, for example, 35 countries had lower child poverty rates than the US. The US was on a par with Mexico and Chile.[2]

When I began looking at this some years ago, it was not uncommon for certain individuals who wanted to deny this reality to say that poverty statistics are based on extreme overestimates of poverty levels among US families and children. The official US poverty threshold

---

1 Poverty in the United State: 2024. U.S. Census Report Number P60-287. Available at: https://www.census.gov/library/publications/2025/demo/p60-287.html.
  Examine the 4th and 7th tables in the Official Poverty Measure list. Also: https://www2.census.gov/library/publications/2025/demo/p60-287.pdf

2 *Society at a Glance 2024: OECD Social Indicators.* Available at: https://www.oecd.org/en/publications/society-at-a-glance-2024_918d8db3-en/full-report/income-poverty_53d4eac1.html#figure-d1e11242-0ee0a256aa

dates back to the late 1950's and is based on the cost of a food basket multiplied by 3, assuming that food expenditures constitute one-third of the living expenses for families. It was regarded as the minimum amount of dollars necessary to meet the needs of the family. The threshold is adjusted for families of differing sizes. Using this measure, the dollar amount designating the poverty threshold has simply been increased based on inflation. For instance, if inflation increased by 2% then the poverty threshold was jacked up by the same amount. Some critics argued that poverty was calculated using an artificial and misleading method because it did not consider the many forms of non-cash assistance for food, housing and other needs that were put in place after 1960. John Iceland in his book *Poverty in America: A Handbook* describes the limitations of the current method in detail. His analysis is informative and worth reading.[3] You can also read in his book about another measure that was based on recommendations made in the 1990's, the SPM or Supplemental Poverty Measure, which takes into account cash income from all sources as well as non-cash assistance. The Census Bureau began calculating and publishing the SPM in 2011. This measure gives the lie to the earlier criticisms because generally the poverty counts under the SPM have been equal to or higher than the official poverty threshold.[4]

We could ask whether either of these measures is a true indicator of the financial needs of US families. Would a family of four (two adults and two children) that earned $100 more than the poverty threshold of $31,200 in 2024 have been substantially better off? They would not be defined as officially poor. We would describe them as near-poor. $31,200 is about 37% of the median income of all U.S. households during 2024: $83,730. The median is the halfway point in a list of all income—half of U.S. families earned more and the other half less than this amount. Could this family of four survive on income just above the official poverty level?

Many families near or below poverty are in jobs earning minimum wage. The level of the minimum wage varies from state to state. It

---

3   John Iceland. (2013). *Poverty in America: A Handbook (Third Edition)*. Berkeley: University of California Press. The relevant materials are in Chapter 2, Methods of Measuring Poverty.

4   U.S. Census Bureau. *Supplemental Poverty Measure*. Available at: census.gov/library/visualizations/ interactive/spm-elements.html Scroll down and look at Tables B-1 and B-2

is easy to show that minimum wage jobs for adults in families with children seldom result in incomes above the poverty level, even when both adults are working. Rather than focusing on minimum wage and poverty levels, a better approach is to ask what kind of pay is needed for families to care for their children and live at least a modest life free from excessive worries about necessities and perhaps with a few luxuries. This has been termed as a *living wage*.

B. Living Wage

A living wage is one that is high enough to cover necessities. Amy Glasmeier of MIT and her colleagues have developed a technique that permits calculation of how large earnings must be in order to be considered a living wage. They present the results for families of different sizes and different numbers of working adults in each county in the United States. Unlike poverty levels which are based on the amount needed to purchase food as a percentage of all earnings, the living wage calculator takes into account the full panoply of fundamental resources necessary to live adequately. These include food, childcare, health, housing, transportation, other necessities, and taxes.[5] Using the federal poverty threshold as an indicator of sufficiency of income is inadequate because that measure does not take into consideration costs such as these. The cost of necessities varies substantially by locality. The living wage calculator takes such differences into account. I present the following as illustrations comparing a few rich, moderate and poor locales (Table 1.1). I have chosen to show families with two adults and two children. The first column shows hourly wages that would be necessary to reach a living wage where both adults are working full-time. The second column shows necessary earnings when only one adult is working. The third column shows earnings at the poverty level. The final column shows the current minimum wage in that county.

---

5   Living Wage Institute. *Living Wage Calculator*. Available at: https://livingwage.mit.edu

Table 1.1. Hourly Living Wage, Poverty Wage, and Minimum Wage for Select U.S. Counties (2/10/2025)				
Richer locales	Living Wage 2 Adults Working	Living Wage 1 Adult Working	Poverty Wage 1 / 2 Working adult(s)	State Minimum Wage
Montgomery County, Maryland	$48.83	$67.36	$12.81/$15.46	$15.00
New York County, New York	$54.74	$68.57	$12.81/$15.46	$15.000
Moderate locales				
St. Louis County, Missouri	$40.87	$51.37	$12.81/$15.46	$13.75
Maricopa County, Arizona	$45.94	$54.80	$12.81/$15.46	$14.70
Poorer locales				
Holmes County, Mississippi	$36.54	$40.01	$12.81/$15.46	$7.25
Claiborne Parish, Louisiana	$35.42	$38.88	$12.81/$15.46	$7.25

What is immediately apparent is that pay necessary to achieve a living wage far exceeds the minimum wage as well as the wages needed to reach the poverty level. Take the example of Claiborne Parish in Louisiana, one of the poorest counties in the United States. A two-parent family in which one adult was working full-time at minimum wage would earn $7.25 per hour, but $38.88 would be needed to reach living wage levels. In Montgomery County, Maryland, one of the richest locales in the US, similar deficiencies are found. A two-parent family in which one adult was working full-time at minimum wage would have $15.00 per hour but pay of $67.36 would be needed to reach living wage levels. These numbers show that earnings in two-adult, two child families in which only one or both are working full-time for minimum wage are woefully inadequate to reach a living wage. Worse results are found for single-parent families. It is easy to see how American families find it impossible to survive in minimum-wage jobs without some further assistance. In addition, families experience great difficulties in many jobs today that pay substantially more than minimum wage.

C. Savings and Debt

Although different statistics are available, fewer than half (46%) of American adults in 2025 had enough savings to cover three months of expenses. A third (33%) had more credit card debt than emergency savings. Nearly a quarter of Americans (24%) had no emergency savings at all.[6]

What this means is that one unexpected expense, say, a large health care bill or car repair or home repair, can sink the family into debt that they often cannot pay off. Debts accumulate on credit cards and grow as exorbitant interest is charged. A 2025 Federal Reserve *Survey of Household Economics and Decision-Making* showed that only 63% of adults said that they could cover a $400 emergency expense. Regarding big current expenses, "Just over half of parents who used paid childcare spent at least 50% as much on childcare as on housing."[7]

A survey by the Kaiser Family Foundation in 2016, *The Burden of Medical Debt,* showed that 41% of adults have health care debt. About 14 million people (6% of adults) in the U.S. owe over $1,000 in medical debt and about 3 million owe more than $10,000.[8]

One of the reasons for this is the astronomical cost of health care in the US. Our for-profit system has resulted in costs that far exceed those of other developed nations. For example, the per capita spending on health care in the US in 2023 averaged $14,570, the highest in world.[9] This amounted to a U.S. total of $4.9 trillion. I will come back to this in later chapters when I examine income disparity and health outcomes and the strange situation in which every developed nation other than the US has universal health care.

---

6   Lane Gillespie. (2025). *Bankrate's 2025 Annual Emergency Savings Report.* Available at: https://www.bankrate.com/banking/savings/emergency-savings-report/

7   Economic Well-Being of U.S. Households in 2024: Fact Sheet. Available at: https://www.federalreserve.gov/newsevents/pressreleases/files/other20250528a1.pdf

8   Shameek Rakshit, Matthew Rae, Gary Claxton, Krutika Amin & Cynthia Cox. (2024). *The Burden of Medical Debt in the United State. Kaiser Family Foundation.* Available at: https://www.healthsystemtracker.org/brief/the-burden-of-medical-debt-in-the-united-states/

9   See Health at a Glance 2023. Available at: https://www.oecd.org/en/publications/health-at-a-glance-2023_7a7afb35-en.html

D. Do Poor Parents Work?

Another criticism of people near or in poverty concerns work. The common misconception is that poor parents do not work. Thus, the reason that people are poor is that they are lazy. By implication, assisting them rewards their laziness. Yet based on 2023 data, about 70% of impoverished U.S. families with children had an adult (sometimes two adults) working at some time during that year.[10] Obviously of course, they did not earn enough to escape poverty. One of the ongoing problems is that many of the children in poverty are of preschool age and the parents can only work if they can find affordable childcare.

The idea of work is a critical one because in our society some of the most important and productive labor is not defined as work because it does not involve a job working for an employer and thus is not worthy of a salary or wage. When we look at the Universal Basic Income (UBI) solution, so-called "women's work," such as child rearing will be considered. What is *work?* This word is horribly limited and biased. However, if you need to be further convinced about work and poverty, I would recommend two older and popular books: *The Working Poor: Invisible in America by David Shipler and Nickel and Dimed: On (Not) Getting by in America* by Barbara Ehrenreich.[11] Both are easy to read and filled with case examples of families trying to survive without a living wage.

Regarding work and poverty, the welfare reform law that was passed in 1996 (known as TANF or Temporary Assistance for Needy Families) restricted the benefits available to participants and the time they could receive them compared to the earlier AFDC (Aid to Families with Dependent Children) program. Notice how the term *children* was dropped from the name. No one in the Clinton administration wanted to be accused of depriving children of their needs, just idle and lazy women. At the same time, recipients of TANF were required to participate in employment and training (E&T) programs. These consisted of job search groups, such as job clubs as well as simply meeting with employment counselors.

---

10   Work and Poverty. Econofact Network. Available at: https://econofact.org/work-and-poverty

11   Barbara Ehrenreich. (2001). *Nickel and Dimed: On (Not) Getting by in America.* New York: Picador Modern Classics; David K. Shipler. (2004). *The Working Poor: Invisible in America.* New York: Random House.

My colleagues and I had some experience with E&T programs of various kinds. We evaluated early Employment and Training (E&T) requirements associated with food stamp (SNAP) programs in Missouri and Iowa. One of the interesting things was that a substantial portion of food stamp recipients were young people temporarily out of work, who found new employment typically in two to three months. Why were federal legislators so abysmally ignorant of the nature of food stamp population when they passed those laws? They seemed to operate more on ideological prejudices than factual data. Reading the testimony and the response of elected representatives at Senate and House hearings before enactment is very enlightening in this regard.

We speculated at the time that the E&T programs would have few beneficial effects. When we were starting the Missouri evaluation, one of us said in a private conversation that it might be more beneficial to take the million dollars that Missouri was allocating to administer the E&T program and drive through poor neighborhoods throwing ten dollar bills out of the car windows. This was suggested as a joke during a meeting that included the head of the agency that administered food tamps. I still remember his head jerk and unamused look. Fortunately, our evaluation research contract was already signed. Yet, when the national evaluation of the food stamp E&T program was later published, no beneficial effects of E&T requirements were found— an example of colossal foolish spending.[12] The same was found in the multiple controlled experiments of welfare reforms in the 1990s. All these efforts stem from the myth that welfare and food stamp recipients are lazy and uninterested in work.

The myth of the lazy, shiftless and irresponsible individuals in our low-income population persists. Its roots stretch back to the English Poor Laws of the early 16th century that provided food, clothing and small amounts of money to the *deserving* poor (such as widows, the elderly and some children). The *undeserving poor* were flogged for begging or were placed in workhouses where their attitudes of laziness and profligacy could be corrected. Unfortunately, workhouses changed nothing. They were just another form of punishment. For a nice short

---

12   Read the abstract of this article: Michael J. Puma & Nancy R. Burstein. (1994). The National Evaluation of the Food Stamp Employment and Training Program. *Journal of Policy Analysis and Management,* 13,2. Available at: https://www.jstor.org/stable/3325016?seq=1#page_scan_tab_contents

history of this concept and its continuation, Part 2 in Philip Jefferson's *Poverty: A Very Short Introduction* is a quick read.[13] But a fuller analysis of the moral dimension of poverty in the US can be found in The *Undeserving Poor: America's Enduring Confrontation with Poverty* by Michael Katz.[14] Katz argues that the idea that poverty results from moral, cultural or biological inadequacies of individual persons has dominated discussions for several hundred years. He also considers other concepts and theories of causes ranging from geography through lack of resources to powerlessness, the evils of capitalism and badly functioning markets.

E. The Upward Mobility Myth

A part of the laziness-industriousness myth is that anyone in America who works hard and has grit can advance their station in life. This is the myth of *upward mobility*, a basic belief of Americans about what is possible in this society. Everyone, we believe, has an equal opportunity to advance in social class. Social class is based on socioeconomic status (SES), which is generally defined on the basis of income, level of education and occupation. So, lower class individuals, usually in or near poverty, can advance to middle class or higher. They only need to apply themselves and work hard. There are some examples of people who have actually done this. You may know people yourself who got a better education, better jobs and made more money than their poor or working-class parents and moved into the middle or upper middle class. Most of these are older folks, however, because upward mobility has become much more difficult today, as numerous analysts have shown. For the first time in US history, a substantial portion of the *millennial* population (born after 1979) will not rise above the SES of the parents and may actually sink below it. Martin Ford deftly summarizes the evidence in his book Rise *of the Robots: Technology and the Threat of a Jobless Future.*[15] Ford notes that this is occurring as a result of seven deadly trends:

---

13   Phillip N. Jefferson. (2018). *Poverty: A Very Short Introduction.* New York: Oxford University Press.

14   Michael B. Katz. (2013). *The Undeserving Poor: America's Enduring Confrontation with Poverty.* New York: Oxford University Press.

15   Martin Ford. (2015). *The Rise of the Robots: Technology and the Threat of a Jobless Future.* New York: Basic Books. The trends referenced are outlined in Chapter 2 of Ford's book.

Wages (in real terms) have been essentially stagnant since 1973.

Corporations' share of the national income has skyrocketed while the share going to laborers has declined sharply, particularly since 2000.

Labor force participation rates have been falling in the past 20-plus years.

Creation of jobs that pay a living wage has declined.

Inequalities in income and wealth have skyrocketed.

College graduates, especially recently, have experienced drops in income and underemployment.

New jobs are more likely to be part-time and in low-wage sectors replacing good paying middle-class jobs.

I would add to this list the burden of nearly $2 trillion in college debt weighing on young people in American society.

A book that contrasts the opportunities for upward mobility of people of the *silent generation* (those born before 1945) with recently born millennials is Our Kids by Robert Putnam.[16] He tells inspiring stories of the lives of old folks graduating high school in the 1950's who were able to advance from poverty to middle class. He also tells depressing stories about the barriers to upward mobility experienced by individuals born more recently.

There are two things I want to emphasize. Millions of American families lack the necessary money to purchase what is needed for millions of American children to live and develop in healthy ways. The problem extends into a large segment of American families and is growing worse. Thus, the large majority of children from the poor through the middle class would benefit from increased money.

The following chapters will consider studies on the effects of financial hardship and poverty on child welfare and development. The literature on this is voluminous. Those who want to educate themselves may read the references that are provided. In each case they will find

---

16   Robert D. Putnam. (2015). *Our Kids: The American Dream in Crisis.* New York: Simon and Schuster. The term silent generation is taken from Paul Taylor's book *The Next America: Boomers, Millennials, and the Looming Generational Showdown.* New York: Public Affairs.

many other citations that if followed will balloon into thousands of articles and books.

Before examining these relationships, a word about study designs is in order.

F. Models and Research Methods

Levels of Explanation. First, concerning possible pathways between money and family/child outcomes, a broad and inclusive model of human behavior is best. There are various more restrictive models that have been used. The *medical model* has often been applied to understanding families. That model in its strictest form assumes that individual behavior and psychological conditions are to be understood and explained primarily in terms of biology. It stresses physiological determinants (genetics, neurophysiology, endocrinology, etc.) of the behavior of parents and children, their interactions, and child development.

Then there are various *psychological models* of human behavior. Some theories (behaviorist, psychoanalytic, developmental, cognitive, etc.) seek to explain behavior primarily in individual terms by considering how behaviors, attitudes, emotions, personalities arise and change. They attend to various kinds of interactions among human beings and between humans and their environments but ultimate explanations for behavior are seen to lie within the bodies and minds of individual people.

Beyond this there are *social psychological models,* where the focus moves out from the individual to consider social interactions between two or more human beings. Interactions of these kinds are treated as complex and real in themselves and not reducible to individual psychology. Finally, there are *sociological and anthropological models* that are focused on large contexts, neighborhoods, entire societies and cultures.

Thousands of books and articles are published each year in these areas. No one can be an expert in more than a small portion of these approaches. However, most of us find it disturbing when someone from one area—say genetics or sociobiology or neurology or personality theory—asserts that studies in his or her area of expertise explain all human development and ongoing behavior. Claims of this kind are disquieting, especially when strong experimental studies can be found in other areas that support equally effective or perhaps better explanations. So, I do not make claims like those in this book. I do not deny the existence and importance of biology, emotions, attitudes, personality, beliefs, social interactions, and the rest. But they are not the focus. They will be treated as intermediate variables that lie between the larger social and economic context, on one side, and on the other side, family and child welfare, parenting, and child development. The question here is whether variables in the larger environment, including the financial capability of families, should be viewed as causes.

Correlational Studies. Scholarly papers based on correlational studies sometimes contain statements to the effect that *correlation does not prove causation*. Each researcher imagines her research methods professor looking stern and wagging her finger and saying, "you can show correlations, but you have to prove causation!" Here is an example, suppose you draw a large sample of adults and collect information on their wealth and their level of education. You find that, on average, the more education individuals have, the greater their wealth. So, you might conclude that education results in (is a causative factor in) acquisition of assets. But is that correct? Someone else might assert that lower wealth restricts educational opportunities, which is not unreasonable when considering generational wealth and inheritance. For example, poorer families have a hard time affording college for their children. Yet another person might say that each of these ideas is wrong and declare that both level of education and amount of wealth are caused by personality factors like determination and true grit. People possessing those characteristics will work to get educated and will also work hard to save their income. Who is right? Further studies of this kind might shed light on the controversy, but we would like to have another method to solve the issue, and that is where experimental designs come in. Nonetheless, correlational studies are invaluable because they shed light on *how questions*.

There are two types of questions: whether and how. The whether-question is most basic. Can we demonstrate that money and the things that money can be used to purchase exert a causal influence on the welfare of families and the development of children? If that can be confirmed then the whether-question can be answered, yes. The how-question concerns models and theories and is about depicting the causal pathways from money to the outcomes of interest. "Okay," someone will say, "you have shown that financial relief has an effect. Can you tell us exactly how such relief produces better outcomes? Can you describe the mechanisms that are involved?" How such effects may be produced is complex as is the production of all outcomes in individual human beings and within social groups. There are often multiple causal paths leading to the same or similar outcomes.

Experimental Approaches. To establish that there is a connection, the *whether*-question is best addressed experimentally. To help in understanding this we present an imaginary world. Imagine for a moment that we live in a universe in which we can rewind and replay history. During Time A, we select a large sample of families and provide them with money and then observe various outcomes for children, say, various measures of physical health. Then we rewind and replay history for this same group. This is Time B. Everything external to families progresses just as before, except in this case we withhold the extra money. We observe the children. If we see differences in our health measures, we can be sure they had to do with the only difference between Time A and Time B: the money provided. How this happened may or may not be answered but whether it happened would have been answered.

The preceding is a fantasy. In the real world, however, we can do the next best thing. We select two groups of families *that are very similar* to one another. There are many ways of doing this. For example, if we start with a large sample of families we might select one of the families as a case for our experimental group and then look closely at all the other families searching for one that is very similar. When found, it would be a matching case to be assigned to our control group. Each time we select and assign an experimental family we search for a similar control family. In this way we build two similar groups of families. In doing this we could use various characteristics, like number of adults and children in the family, their various ages, marital status and history, the type of neighborhood they live in, their extended family, and so on. The list of these can be as long as we want, although the more characteristics that are considered the harder it is to find a close match on all of them. Nonetheless, this can and has been done in some studies. For instance, I describe field experiments in Chapter 4 that involved matched children and families. The matching child or family for each experimental case is then placed in a comparison group that acts as a control.

Once the experimental and control groups are assembled the field researchers provide an intervention (money or material resources) to the experimental families. This is usually called the *experimental treatment*. The intervention is *not provided* to the control group families. Then during a follow-up period, the researchers observe the outcomes among the children in each group for any differences in their welfare or development.

This kind of design is not perfect. In matching, there are always other characteristics that might have been used for matching but were not, and it is possible that unbeknownst to the matchers they were very important and might be implicated in any differences between the children that were measured. Nonetheless, if carefully carried out, matching studies can provide compelling proof of the whether-question.

There are other kinds of quasi-experimental designs that utilized alternative methods of selecting similar control groups. For instance, there are other ways of matching and there are other methods utilizing various statistical procedures.

The best designs utilize random *assignment,* also called *randomized control trial (RCT)* studies. In this case, the decision to assign a family to the experimental or control group is based on a flip of the coin: heads the family is in the experimental group, tails it is in the control group. The coin flip is usually accomplished through a randomizing function in a computer program. This procedure tends to produce virtually identical groups of families, if the groups are relatively large, say 150 cases or more. Properly assigned, the group will be very similar in statistical averages, such as average age of parents, average family size, proportions of male and female children, proportions of mother-only families, etc. Pick a characteristic and you will find similar averages or proportions. An exercise in research methods classes is to give students a large data set with various characteristics of individual cases and have them assign the cases randomly to two separate groups and then compare the groups. Surprise, they will be nearly identical on all dimensions. Nonetheless, comparisons of many relevant characteristics are often presented in RCT reports to convince readers that this actually is the case. Because of this similarity, when the experimental treatment is applied and differences are later observed, we can be confident that the treatment *caused* them to occur.

Experimental designs may be prospective in nature. The groups are set up at one point in time and the experimental treatment and observations or measurements take place subsequently. But sometimes experimental designs may look backward. These are *retrospective*, studying large sets of existing data on families and children, designating experimental and control cases and then looking for differences in outcomes. I will describe a study we conducted that utilized such a design.

The observations and measurements conducted in some experiments may give us information on how differences occurred. This may or may not be the case, depending on the study design and measurements. Nonetheless, when experiments are properly designed and competently conducted they can be appealed to as evidence that the treatment—in this book, additional money or resources provided to families with children—produced the differences between experimental and control children. The *whether*-question is confirmed even though *how*-questions may be only partly answered.

The Complexity of the "How" Question. The problem with the question of how families and children might be affected by increases or decreases in money is that characteristics (variables) at the different levels mentioned above from biological to environmental may come into play. Take the example of job loss of a parent resulting in reduction of family income for several months. One of the results for some people depending both on their biology, their emotional history, and their coping skills is increased stress. We can think of this as a risk resulting from income reduction, where risk means the *probability or* *likelihood* that psychological and physical tension that we call stress will result from reduction in income. Overall, reduction in income is correlated with an increase in stress, but this varies from person to person. When it occurs, increased and prolonged stress is itself a risk factor for a variety of negative behavioral and emotional responses, which are also quite variable. One person increases alcohol intake and is regularly drunk. Another becomes unable to control anxiety and weeps incessantly. Yet another has episodes of sudden and extreme anger in response to otherwise minor events. This person sinks into a state of clinical depression. That person moves out of the home, abandoning the family. We might, in fact, develop *risk* probabilities for these kinds of responses. Some of these may then in turn increase the risk of over-severe physical discipline of children or spending less time talking to them or ignoring their hygiene or their whereabouts during the day or evening or neglecting to assist them with their schoolwork or other negative behaviors. These sequences have been referred to as *risk chains*, and you can surmise that there are many and they are incredibly varied. Another risk from loss of income and stress in two adult households is marital discord involving arguing and accusations about relationships and resources. This may result in domestic violence in some families. In others it is a risk factor for separation and divorce. These changes then may affect the children in various negative ways, another set of risk chains. Then imagine an increase in money. This may lower the risk of stress and increase the probability of contentment and lead to greater attention to the child and in turn to improvements in the child's behavior and school performance. We will look briefly at studies of such chains.

Chapter 2

How Financial Hardship Threatens Families and Children

A. Case Study Illustrations

Here are several case-study examples illustrating how financial hardship and poverty may affect the welfare of children. These are taken from studies of child maltreatment that my colleagues and I conducted.

Case Study 1. This case arose from a report that two younger children (ages 3 and 5 years) were being cared for by a preteen child (age 10). After an investigation, it was substantiated as lack of proper supervision. The mother had recently lost her job and was suffering from depression. The family was currently living on the social security check that came to the older child, whose father had died the year before. When I visited the family with a service worker, the mother expressed guilt about using her daughter's check for food and rent. She had no alternative for childcare when she had to go out. Limited resources were a major part of the problem leading to the finding of lack of proper supervision.

The following case illustrates how depression, stress and poverty may interact in a family. This was voluntary case that we followed.

Case Study 2. A referral was made by another agency for a young woman, who was requesting services. She had worked with the county previously and requested a specific worker, as she felt comfortable with her. She had just had a baby and was feeling overwhelmed financially and emotionally. She had recently begun working at a local grocery store but was still relying on welfare (TANF). In addition, she had been diagnosed with post-traumatic stress disorder, depression, and anxiety. She wanted help with parenting initially, but the PSOP worker primarily intervened to help manage crises that arose. The young woman had trouble maintaining employment. Indeed, she lost two jobs during the case period. She had several barriers to becoming financially independent: no high school diploma, no driver's license, no vehicle, no child support, and trouble with childcare. The voluntary program was able to assist with rent, utilities, and other basic needs for a month. Her infant son had also been hospitalized twice in the previous month for a medical condition. The worker helped her think about how to manage the child's condition. She also encouraged her to work on developing her parenting skills. She and the worker developed a monthly budget. She was referred to a mental health agency for long-term help. Chemical use was also a possible issue, and she was provided with some education on substance abuse. A home-based worker was recruited for the case to work more directly on mental health and parenting, and this allowed the worker to focus more on coordination and case management. During the case, a report was received regarding the mother's behavior and parenting, but nothing new or substantial was reported. Later, she became pregnant again and began having domestic incidents with her new boyfriend. However, she did secure employment and began to attend individual counseling. The workers continued to address the goals of safety, budgeting, and home management. The case was closed by mutual agreement after the mother felt she had adequate access to other services and was satisfied with her current situation.

The following is a case of a drug-addicted mother. It was part of an observational study that we conducted. The report was made by a policeman. A formal child abuse and neglect investigation was conducted resulting in the removal and placement of her children into relative care.

Case Study 3. An anonymous report was received that a mother had left her five children alone from 7:00 a.m. to 7:00 p.m. This was a mother-only family, as she was separated from the father of the children. The mother told the children that she was going to the grocery store, but when she returned, she had no groceries, because she had sold her food stamps for cash to buy drugs. The reporter said that the children were left alone often and that the two youngest (ages one and two) usually played alone outside. The electricity had been turned off in the house the day before.

Following the investigation, a maternal aunt of the children took them in, but two more hotline reports were received two days later. The first may have been from the aunt, who reported that the children's maternal grandmother had come that morning and picked them up. The reporter claimed that the grandmother was not physically capable of caring for the children. The second hotline was from a policeman who was at the grandmother's home, saying that immediate action was needed because the mother was at the grandmother's home. She wanted to take the children, although she had no money, no food, and no home. The local shelters were not a resource, because the mother was on drugs and was extremely high at the time. The policeman confirmed that the mother had used all her welfare and food stamps to buy drugs. The policeman arrested the mother and took her to the county jail. He also took the children into protective custody and transported them to the family court. The investigator went to the family court, met the children, and interviewed them with a juvenile officer. They found the children highly active but unresponsive to adults. All the children were aware that their mother had spent all the family's money on drugs and showed detailed knowledge of buying and using dope. Together the investigator and juvenile officer decided to place the three youngest children with the mother's sister and the two oldest children with their father. Whether the placement with the father was wise is debatable since we later heard that he was a drug dealer who had supplied the drugs to mother as she became addicted. However, this was hearsay. This arrangement was approved by the juvenile court, and at the detention hearing, custody and control was given to the child welfare agency. The investigator completed her report with a formal finding of child neglect.

About three months later, I accompanied the foster care worker and the children on a visit to the mother at a drug rehabilitation center. The mother had voluntarily agreed to undergo drug treatment and was doing well. She was well dressed and cheerful. The children obviously loved their mother and were taking turns being held. Later she was released and regained custody of her children.

This case illustrates how poverty and other mediating variables may interact. Whether and how poverty might have been involved in creating her addiction is unknown. That problem may have been more attributable to the influence of the children's father, but we did not confirm that. After the mother was addicted, her need for drugs contributed to her financial distress. Had she not been addicted she would probably have been simply another poor single mother. In this case, unlike many we have observed, she had the advantage of a supportive extended family that helped during her rehab.

Here is another case in which funds were used to prevent removal and placement of children. It was part of the Indiana IV-E project, discussed in Chapter 4.

Case Study 4. A report came from the police regarding lack of supervision. A maintenance man who came to fix the stove reported finding a two-year-old child alone in the apartment. The mother arrived an hour later and stated that she had gone to the Trustee's office for some financial help and did not want to wake her child. She had left him alone with safety gates on the bedroom door and admitted to previously having left the child alone on several occasions. The report was substantiated, and a short-term Informal Adjustment case was opened.

The family consisted of a single mother and her two-year old son who was developmentally disabled. It appeared that the family was struggling financially, was socially isolated and that the mother was depressed. The mother had been unemployed for the past two months, in part due to attending to the disabilities of her child. During those two months, the child had undergone two surgeries for clubfoot. The mother had been employed full-time prior to the operations, but she was forced to quit her job when she could not secure extended leave. The lack of regular income threatened imminent homelessness for the family. They did not have any family support in the area. The family had no prior history with the Missouri Department of Children's Services.

The mother agreed to cooperate with a parent aide and an in-home therapist, accepted home visits from First Steps, properly supervise her son, obtain adequate medical care, and administer medication he needed. Although the mother had two job prospects, she was waiting for appropriate daycare for her son. Past rent in the amount of $677 was owed and the family was facing eviction. Despite support from Section 8, she had accrued a large past due balance on her rent, including late fees and eviction filing fees. The woman was provided with financial help for rent assistance, vouchers for daycare, counseling, and an in-home parent aide. The parent aide helped the mother with budgeting, looking for work and locating the nearest food pantry. The mother was compliant with DCS and all service providers. The waiver utilization included $5,912 for rent assistance, home-based counseling and parent aide.

The case was assigned to waiver status to assist the family maintain its housing and avoid eviction. Without this assistance, the family might have lost the apartment, and the case could easily have risen to a removal and placement due to the child's special needs. The mother successfully completed 90-days of in-home therapy and parent aide sessions. Great progress was made, and the assigned therapist concluded that the mother did not need continued services. All the child's doctor's appointments were successfully attended and the mother also obtained consistent daycare. At case closure, the mother was employed, and she and her child were living in a stable environment.

Here is another case of homelessness, something we observed in large numbers in the impoverished Mississippi counties in the IV-E study described in the Chapter 4. Note here the reference to disabilities and frequent moves as direct causes.

Case Study 5. This case involved a two-parent family with an 11-year-old son and a 14-year-old daughter. The father was disabled and unable to work and the family had a history of instability and frequent moves that led to serious behavioral and emotional problems for the children. The family became homeless when they were unable to pay their rent and were forced out of their home. The children were taken into custody and placed in foster care, but the placement situations were unreliable. Through the waiver, the family received short-term assistance to pay rent, and the parents found new living arrangements that allowed the son to live with them once again. Waiver funds were also used to pay for tutoring services for the boy to help him catch up for missed time at school. A placement with relatives was secured for the daughter through waiver funds which paid for a bed and medication prescribed to address her bouts of severe anxiety. Finally, the mother was helped to find a job and the family attained a level of stability it had lacked for several years.

As noted, cases of extreme poverty were common in this and other studies we conducted. The approach was to try to meet basic and home-related needs so that children did not have to be removed and placed in foster care. Here is another example that would seem to fall into the category of poverty misinterpreted as child neglect.

Case Study 6. The case involved a woman with four children between the ages 3 and 9. A boyfriend of the woman lived with her from time to time and was the father of the children, but he did not provide a steady source of financial support. A child protection case was opened on the family after the utilities had been turned off and there was little food in the house. To forestall the removal of the children until the situation could be more permanently addressed, waiver funds were used to purchase food and pay the utility bills so that power, heat, and water could be restored to the home.

The stop-gap nature of this case was replicated in many other cases we followed. The following is an example of the use of IV-E waiver funds and the hard work of a wonderful worker to assist in family reunification. Direct causes in this case means 'low functioning' parents.

Case Study 7. This example involved the case of a young family with low-functioning parents and three children aged 2, 7 and 9 years. The family had been homeless until a brother gave them a small mobile home to use. But the trailer was unsafe and did not have functioning sanitary or electrical systems. The children were taken into custody, removed, and placed in foster care for neglect. The foster home was 100 miles from the parents; no closer foster placement could be found that would accept all three children. Waiver and county funds were used to purchase needed materials to repair the trailer. The parents took an active hand in the process and repaired the windows and fixed the leaking roof and had a septic tank installed. The county social worker, showing extraordinary commitment to her case family, laid the plumbing and did all the needed electrical work herself during her off hours. Once repairs were completed, the Juvenile Court judge allowed the children to be released from paid foster care and reunited with their parents.

In the following three sections, studies of the effects of financial stress are examined in somewhat greater detail. The first is food and diet. These are studies considering how financial hardship might lead to nutritional problems in children. The second area concerns housing. Poverty and financial problems can and do result in poor housing and homelessness. The third concerns the situation of single parent families headed by women, so called mother-only families. In the final section family stress is examined as a cause.

B. Enough Food and a Healthy Diet

In 2016, 16.5% of US households with children under age 18 were *food insecure* at some time during the year, based on a yearly USDA survey of American families. Again, this is one of those astounding statistics, like child poverty, that most Americans find hard to believe. How is this even possible in a society that throws away nearly half of all produce or one-third of all food? There is an interesting old article in *The Atlantic* (drawing from a reference in *The Guardian* newspaper) arguing that this amounts to about 60 million tons a year costing $160 billion.[17] Food insecure families most often reported not having enough money in a given month to get food when it was running out and being unable to afford balanced meals and being worried about food running out. In some cases, they reported that their children were not eating enough because the family could not afford enough food.[18] Not having enough money leads to reductions in food expenditure and thus in the quantity of food available. Just as importantly, inadequate food

---

17   Adam Chandler. (2016). Why America Leads the World in Food Waste. *The Atlantic*, July 15, 2016. https://www.theatlantic.com/business/archive/2016/07/american-food-waste/491513/

18   Alisha Coleman-Jensen, Matthew P. Rabbitt, Christian A. Gregory & Anita Singh. (2017). *Household Food Security in the United States in 2016*. Economic Research Report Number 237, Economic Research Service. U.S. Department of Agriculture. Available at: https://www.ers.usda.gov/webdocs/publications/84973/err-237.pdf?v=0

expenditures lead to poorer diets overall, including diets of children. For example, another study of food stamp (SNAP) recipients by Mabli and associates found that greater cash for food expenditures was directly related to the quality of the diet. This included increased intake of healthy foods and reduction of unhealthy foods and an increase of foods with greater nutrient density.[19]

The increase in food insecurity brought on by the 2020-22 COVID-19 pandemic was partially addressed through legislation specifying a 15% increase in SNAP benefits through September of 2020. By December, a much smaller package contained $13 billion in nutrition assistance increasing the maximum allotments of SNAP to families. This kind of assistance should be extended permanently.

More money equals more and better food in families and for children. A better diet means better overall health and perhaps reduced obesity, a major problem of both children and adults in the US. But inadequate and unhealthy diets also affect children's learning ability and behavior.

The causal pathways between food and child welfare are many. For example, unbalanced diets are associated with chronic childhood illnesses and poor school achievement. Here is a good illustrative study: *Associations between Household Food Insecurity in Early Childhood and Children's Kindergarten Skills* by Anna Johnson and Anna Markowitz. The authors reference scores of earlier research reports on this topic, and of course, an extensive literature also exists produced by nutritionists supporting the relationship between balanced diets and healthy brain development.[20]

Johnson and Markowitz studied a recent (2001) large birth cohort of thousands of children from 96 US counties or county clusters looking at the relationship between food insecurity of children (at ages 9 months, 2 years and preschool age) and kindergarten reading

---

19   James Mabli, Laura Castner, James Ohls, Mary Kay Fox, Mary Kay Crepinsek & Elizabeth Condon. (2010). *Food Expenditures and Diet Quality among Low-Income Households and Individuals.* Washington, D.C.: Mathematica Policy Research. Available at: https://www.mathematica-mpr.com/our-publications-and-findings/publications/food-expenditures-and-diet-quality-among-lowincome-households-and-individuals

20   Anna D. Johnson & Anna J. Markowitz. (2018). Associations between Household Food Insecurity in Early Childhood and Children's Kindergarten Skills. *Child Development*, 89,2, e1-e17.

and math skills, hyperactivity, conduct problems and approaches to learning. They found: Food insecurity in 20% of children at some time throughout their early childhood.

Notice that this is greater than 16.5% each year, cited above. It is reminiscent of substantially higher rates of child poverty at any time during childhood years compared to rates during only one year. Food insecurity was related to poor socio-emotional outcomes such as:

- *Hyperactivity* (e.g., how well a child pays attention, resists distraction, sits still),

- *Conduct problems* (e.g., how often a child pushes another person or throws tantrums), and

- *Approaches to learning* (e.g., how focused, independent and eager to learn).

They also found an association with *math and reading skills,* which appeared to be most strongly related to children in a category they created and titled *very-low* food security.

Depriving children of sufficient food and balanced diets results in lasting negative consequences in their lives.

C. Housing

My colleagues and I saw hundreds of cases of poor and substandard housing that were representative of many reports of child neglect among the thousands of families studied in several U.S. states. Readers may peruse our website (www.iarstl.org) for scores of case examples in our studies of child welfare programs in eight US states.[21] Six of these are summarized in Chapter 4. The studies demonstrate that assistance with housing including back rent, utilities, working with landlords, repair of dilapidated homes, and so on, in the context of broader material support, can lead to reductions in later reports of child maltreatment. Other examples can be found in Matthew Desmond's book: *Evicted: Poverty and Profit in the American City.*[22]

---

21   The studies involved multi-method, multi-year evaluation research in Missouri, Minnesota, Nevada, Ohio, Mississippi, Indiana, Maryland and Washington, DC. Together these studies examined more than 20,000 families.

22   Matthew Desmond. (2016). *Evicted: Poverty and Profit in the American City.* New York: Crown Publishers.

Homelessness in the U.S. Another indicator of the extent of the housing problem in the U.S. is homelessness. On a single night in 2024, there were 771,480 individuals experiencing homelessness. Of these, over a third (35.5%) were unsheltered. About one in five (18.9%) of the total homeless were children, 17 years old or younger. Safe, clean and affordable housing can and should be easily available to every U.S. family.[23]

The 2020-22 pandemic brought to light the special needs of this population. As the National Alliance website indicated: "Self-quarantine, social isolation, and stay-at-home orders are difficult, if not impossible, to follow when you do not have a home." The Alliance cited research that demonstrates how shelters should be expanded to accommodate social distancing among the currently sheltered population and additional shelters for the unsheltered. An estimated 400,000 additional shelter units would be needed nationally.[24]

Rent Assistance. One of the reasons for evictions and homelessness is the shortage of affordable rental housing. There were 43.3 million renter households in the US in 2017. Eleven million (25.4%) of the total renter households had exceptionally low incomes. Assuming that households should not spend more than 30% of their income on housing, only 7.4 million rental homes were available and affordable to households in this category. The shortage in that year, therefore, amounted to 3.6 million homes. None of the 50 states had an adequate supply of rental housing for the lowest income renters.[25] One of the causes of homelessness is eviction when families are unable to pay rent.

Is inadequate housing related to the welfare of children? The following is an example study of the effects of substandard housing on children. It is a paper by Rebekah Coley and associates: *Relations between Housing Characteristics and the Well-Being of Low-Income*

---

23   These statistics come from the Congressional Research Services report, Homelessness, published in May 2025 and available at: https://www.congress.gov/crs-product/IF12985

24   Dennis Culhane, Dan Treglia, Ken Steif, Randall Kuhn & Thomas Byrne. (March *2020*). *Estimated Emergency and Observational/Quarantine Capacity Need for the US Homeless Population Related to COVID-19 Exposure by County; Projected Hospitalizations, Intensive Care Units and Mortality.* University of Pennsylvania. Available at: https://endhomelessness.org/wp-content/uploads/2020/03/COVID-paper_clean-636pm.pdf

25   Andrew Aurand, Dan Emmanuel, Ellen Errico, Dina Pinsky & Diane Yentel. (2019). *The Gap, A Shortage of Affordable Homes.* National Low Income Housing Coalition. Available at: https://reports.nlihc.org/sites/default/files/gap/Gap-Report_2019.pdf

Children and Adolescents.[26] Like our previous example of inadequate food and nutrition, this study is abundantly referenced. Coley et al. followed a cohort of 2,437 children and adolescents from low-income urban neighborhoods in three cities over time. The advantage of this study over previous research is that it considered various housing features:

- The physical *quality of the housing* (structural, maintenance and problems such as a leaking roof, broken windows, rodents, inoperative stoves, peeling paint, exposed wiring, etc.),

- *housing type* (assisted housing, rented or owned),

- *residential instability* (whether the family had moved in the previous year), and

- *housing cost burden* (total housing cost including utilities as a proportion of total household income).

This enabled the researchers to determine which features of housing were related to various developmental outcomes of children. These included anxiety, depression, withdrawal, somatic complaints, aggression, and rule breaking behavior. Reading and math skills were also assessed. Various family characteristics were measured and utilized in the analysis along with family functioning measures including the psychological distress of mothers. They found that housing quality was most important. Children in lower quality housing showed:

- Greater emotional and behavioral problems compared to those in higher quality homes. As housing problems increased over time, emotional and behavioral problems correspondingly increased.

- Reduced cognitive (reading and math) skills. How might this occur? The authors speculate that stress may be involved. They also consider health problems, such as those resulting from exposure to lead paint, asthma and allergies. Further,

---

26   Rebekah Levine Coley, Tama Leventhal, Alicia Doyle Lynch & Milissa Kull. (2012). Relations between Housing Characteristics and the Well-Being of Low-Income Children and Adolescents. *Developmental Psychology*, 49,9. 1775-1789.

conditions like lack of heat, hot water or adequate lighting could affect learning and social activities.

- Poorer psychological functioning of the mother was found to be an important intervening factor.

Another large-scale study by Dominique Goux and Eric Maurin in France considered overcrowding, *The Effect of Overcrowded Housing on Children's Performance in School.*[27] They found a strong association between overcrowding and academic failure. They noted that children in large families did more poorly than children in smaller families, although the reason for this was not family size itself but that overcrowding occurs more often in larger families. This is another reason why the dropout rate of children living in or near poverty is significantly higher in the US. The event dropout rate refers to the percentage of youths in grades 10 through 12 who leave high school between the beginning of one school year and the beginning of the next without earning a high school diploma or an alternative credential such as a GED (high school equivalency diploma). This rate was 7.2% and 5.3% respectively in 2016 for the lowest quarter and the middle low quarter of family incomes compared to 3.6% and 3.9% for the higher quarters.[28]

D. Mother-Only Families

The sociological term for this is family structure, which for our purposes refers to single-parent versus two-parent families. The large majority of single-parent families are female headed, meaning mother-only. A long-term research project called the Fragile Families and Child Wellbeing Study has considered the plight of children in these two different family structures. A summary of research findings from this study in the late 1990's through 2009 is summarized in *Fragile Families and Child Wellbeing* by Jane Waldfogel and associates.[29] They demonstrated that: Children in mother-only families have poorer

---

27   Dominique Goux & Eric Maurin. (2005). The Effect of Overcrowded Housing on Children's Performance in School. *Journal of Public Economics*, 89, 797-819.

28   National Center for Educational Statistics. (2017). Trends in High School Dropout and Completion Rates in the United States. Available at: https://nces.ed.gov/programs/dropout/ind_01.asp

29   Jane Waldfogel, Terry Ann Craigie & Jeanne Brooks Gunn. (2010). Fragile Families and Child Wellbeing. *The Future of Children* 20(2):87-112. Available at: https://www.ncbi.nlm.nih.gov/pmc/articles/PMC3074431/pdf/nihms-273444.pdf

outcomes as they grow up than children in two-parent families. For our purposes here, a major factor is that mother-only families have fewer material resources.

- The mother's mental health, especially depression, was an intervening variable, increasing negative outcomes. Family stability, which refers to a child growing up with the same parent, versus instability, living under two different parents, is also an issue. The research shows:

Negative behavioral effects for children living in mother-only families versus cognitive and health problems for children in unstable family structures.

Lee Dahoon and Sara McLanahan considered transitions between different family structures and looked at differences by racial/ethnic identity.[30]

The effects of transitions is something I and my associated examined for these two different family structures, as we studied families reported multiple times for child maltreatment.[31] Our analysis examined cohorts of families. Some maintained the same structure over time; they remained mother-only or two-adult. Others changed from mother-only to two-adult or vice versa. We showed that transitions to mother-only status resulted in reduced employment, and by implication reductions in income. This in turn led to increases in child neglect reports. We argue below that many child neglect reports are not intentional neglect of children but societal neglect of families in poverty that comes to be labeled as neglect of children.

Speaking of transitions, we can ask why the transitions from two-parent to single-parent status are so much more frequent in the United States than in other developed countries. Andrew Cherlin in *The Marriage-Go-Round* notes that after only five-years more than one in five Americans who had married were either separated or divorced.

---

30   Lee Dohoon & Sara McLanahan. (2015). Family Structure Transitions and Child Development: Instability, Selection and Population Heterogeneity. *American Sociological Review, 80(4),* 738-763. McLanahan is the Princeton sociologist who has directed the Fragile Families studies for many years.

31   L. Anthony Loman. (2006). *Families Frequently Encountered in Child Protection Services: A Report on Chronic Child Abuse and Neglect.* Institute of Applied Research. The relevant analyses can be found on pages 30-34. Available at: http://www.iarstl.org/papers/FEfamiliesChronicCAN.pdf

This is twice the rate in other western nations. Even more alarming is the rate of breakup of cohabiting unmarried couples, which amounts to more than 50% over five years. Again, this is substantially higher than other western nations. American children are more likely to live through such a breakup than are children in most other countries—about three quarters by age 15. Since in most of these cases another partner enters the picture, American children are more likely to experience a third adult in their household.[32] Look back at the aforementioned findings regarding cognitive and health problems of children in unstable family structures. Cherlin includes an interesting comparison with Sweden noting the children born in married families in the US are more likely to experience a parental breakup than children born to cohabiting parents in Sweden. The reasons for these differences are beyond the scope of this book, but we would ask whether and to what extent the declining fortunes of laborers in the United States might be a factor in the breakup of relationships. Paul Taylor presents a good summary of theories concerning these issues in Chapter 9 of his book *The Next America*.[33]

E. Family Stress

In what way can family financial hardship and poverty be thought of as a cause of failures in child safety and welfare? There is a complex sense in which something can be a cause. I use the term *moderating cause*. In this model, some characteristic of a child or parent or family context is worsened because of the stress of financial hardship.

Rand Conger and Katherine Conger have outlined a causal sequence that illustrates the moderating cause process more fully, which they name The Family Stress Model.[34] The model includes the following:

1. *Economic hardship* (low income, high debt, low assets, and negative financial events) leads to:

---

32   Andrew J. Cherlin. (2009). *The Marriage-Go-Round*. New York: Vintage Books.

33   Paul Taylor. (2015). *The Next America: Boomers, Millennials and the Looming Generational Showdown*. New York: PublicAffairs.

34   Rand Conger & Katherine Conger. (2008). Understanding the Processes through which Economic Hardship Influences Families and Children. Chapter 5 in *Handbook of Families and Poverty*, ed. Crane, D., & Heaton, T. Los Angeles: Sage Publications.

2. *Economic pressure* (unmet material needs, unpaid debts and painful cutbacks). These in turn lead to:

3. *Parent distress* (emotional and behavioral problems), which produces:

4. *Disrupted family relations* (inter-parental conflict or withdrawal and harsh or inconsistent parenting). Finally, this produces:

5. *Child and adolescent adjustments* (emotional problems, behavioral problems and impaired competence).

The Rands also present the obverse of the stress model: *The Family Resource Model.* In that model family resources and the lack thereof are predicted to affect child outcomes. There are resources that are only indirectly related to finances but the critical ones such as health, education, housing, living arrangements, transportation, leisure activities, neighborhoods, safety, etc. are clearly produced or directly affected by income and wealth. Some instances of this are considered in the following sections of this chapter.

The family stress model predicts that such hardship may exacerbate negative traits of caregivers and children. These are destructive behaviors and harmful human relationships that directly cause child maltreatment. On the other hand, the model predicts that sufficient money makes the expression of positive traits, supportive behaviors and beneficial relationships more likely.

A study by Mi-Youn Yang shows the effects of relationship between material hardship, parent psychological states on investigated reports of child maltreatment among families receiving cash welfare.[35] Material hardship was measured in four areas: sufficient food, adequate housing and homelessness, problems with utilities, and medical deficiencies. Yang demonstrated the correlation between future investigations of child maltreatment and problems in any one of these areas. The correlation was stronger when hardship was experienced in two or more areas. The study demonstrates the relationship of parental stress and depressive symptoms arising from material hardship on later

---

35   Mi-Youn Yang. (2015). The effect of material hardship on child protective service involvement. *Child Abuse & Neglect*, 41, pages 113-125.

reports, as well. Discussions of food insecurity, inadequate housing, and homelessness are further discussed below.

Another paper that focused on family income and child welfare by Greg Duncan and associates considered how economic disadvantage leads to stress in families and in turn affects the development of children.[36]

A recent study by Yiran Zhang and associates used a large sample of families to test the family stress model. They found direct effects on paternal depression and psychological aggression.[37] For those who wish to immerse themselves further in the literature on this topic these studies are abundantly referenced.

---

36   Duncan G.J., Magnuson K., Votruba-Drzal E. 2014. Boosting family income to promote child development. *The Future of Children*, 24(1): 99–120. Available at: https://escholarship.org/uc/item/5rv2k936

37   Yiran Zhang, Michelle Johnson-Motoyama, Susan Yoon & Gia Barboza-Salerno. (2025). From material hardship to harsh parenting: Testing the Family Stress Model in dyadic family context. *Public Health*, 248, 105917.

Chapter 3

What is Child Maltreatment?

In the next chapter six studies that I and my associates conducted will be considered. They demonstrate the positive effects of provision of money and material resources on families suffering financial hardship. The studies focused on services to families reported for maltreating their children. Thus, as a first step we should take a look at definitions of child maltreatment.

A. Kinds of Child Maltreatment

When we began studying child maltreatment in Missouri in the 1990's, the state already had a comprehensive computer data system documenting thousands of child protection cases. As we received copies of the database, we were able to review the kinds of actions and situations that were being reported. We did an early analysis based on over 51,000 CA/N reports received in the early-1990's. We grouped similar allegations together and counted the times they occurred. Proportions were based on counts of reports that included particular allegations. Thus, they add to more than 100% since multiple allegations of various kinds may be made in the same report.

We classified the following as severe physical abuse: allegations of internal injuries, bone fractures, subdural hemorrhage/hematoma, skull fractures, brain damage, dismemberment, child fatality. What we found at that time was that these kinds of accusations occurred in less than 1% of total reports. When we added in claims involving wounds, cuts and punctures (all reported about the same child), along with exposure, freezing, heat exhaustion, child abandonment and failure to thrive, the proportion increased to 5.5% of total reports. Reports containing sexual abuse allegations included sexually transmitted disease, fondling, touching, oral sex, sodomy, digital penetration, intercourse, genital or anal bleeding, pornography, and an undefined category of other sexual abuse. These were found in 10.2% of reports. By adding these all together the proportion of reports with highly dangerous and damaging allegations rose to 15.7%. The percentage of very dangerous allegations is somewhat greater because some of the reports in other categories, if true, represented serious threats to child safety.

The majority of reports involved accusations of child neglect, such as lack of supervision, lack of food, lack of or inappropriate clothing, poor hygiene, lack of heat, unsafe or inadequate shelter, unsanitary living conditions, lack of concern for children's education (educational neglect), various types of medical neglect, such as an untreated illness or failure to give a child prescribed medications. Together allegations of these kinds constituted about two-thirds of the total count. Some 20% of the reports included less severe physical abuse, mainly bruises, welts or red marks, often from over-severe physical discipline. There were also many allegations of conflicts within families (in about one in every three reports) that were more often associated with teenage children. They included things like expelling from home, locking in or out, verbal abuse, and the like.

We found this pattern to be roughly consistent across subsequent multi-method, multi-year studies in six states. For example, in a more recent study in Washington, D.C., completed in 2016, we found, like the old Missouri analysis, that allegations of inadequate shelter, inadequate food or nutrition, poor clothing or hygiene, lack of supervision, educational neglect and various types of medical neglect constituted about two thirds of all allegations received, while again very serious and damaging reports were a small minority.[38]

B. Economic hardship, Poverty and Child Maltreatment

What are the families like that are reported for child maltreatment? They have diverse problems and deficiencies, but in our studies we have found that families and children reported for child abuse and neglect

---

38   The full report of the 2016 study is available at http://www.iarstl.org/papers/FinalReportCFSA-DC. pdf.

(CA/N) and in open child welfare cases are usually poor, ranging from near-poverty levels to financially destitute. This has been confirmed in nationwide studies over several decades. It was found again in the Fourth National Incidence Study (NIS) of Child Abuse and Neglect in 2010 in which Sedlak and associates drew a large representative sample of families from child welfare data systems across the nation.[39] They measured low socioeconomic status (SES) by combining measures of levels of income and education as well as participation in poverty programs. In the national study, low SES children (i.e., those living in families in or in danger of poverty) were approximately five times more likely to experience maltreatment than children who were not in low SES families.

This is consistent with our findings. For instance, in the study in Ohio summarized in the next chapter, we found that nearly seven out of ten surveyed families reported for child maltreatment had 2008 incomes of $15,000 or less compared to approximately 8% of all Ohio families. Similar results were observed in Minnesota in the sixth study of the Parent Support Outreach Program (PSOP) summarized below.[40] When PSOP workers assessed the financial condition of the families that accepted services, they found that 60% had inadequate incomes or were in poverty. In about 14%, the poverty was extreme and severe. The consistent evidence is that families encountered by child protection agencies are the poorest families in our society.

Families reported several times tend to be the poorest of the poor. For example, a Minnesota study we conducted examined the risk of child abuse and neglect among families reported to the child protection agency.[41] Workers who observed and interviewed family caregivers completed items that have been shown to be predictive of future child abuse or neglect. One of those was situations of severe financial difficulties. Families were rated as experiencing such financial

---

39   Andrea J. Sedlak, Jane Mettenburg, Monica Basena, Ian Petta, Karla McPherson, Angela Greene & Spencer Li. (2010). Fourth national incidence study of child abuse and neglect (NIS-4): Report to Congress. Washington, DC: U.S. Department of Health and Human Services, Administration for Children and Families. Available at: https://www.acf.hhs.gov/sites/default/files/opre/nis4_report_exec_summ_pdf_jan2010.pdf

40   Full report available at http://www.iarstl.org/papers/PSOPFinalReport.pdf. The chart of interest here is on page 37.

41   L. Anthony Loman & Gary L. Siegel. (2004). *An evaluation of Minnesota SDM family risk assessment: Final report.* Available at: http://www.iarstl.org/papers/FinalFRAReport.pdf

problems when they could not consistently pay for one or more basic necessities, such as rent, heat, lights, food or clothing. When financial strain was measured at the time of the first report on the family, almost twice as many families who were subsequently reported three or more times (21%) were in severe financial difficulty compared to families with fewer or no later reports (12%). This is considered along with data from other studies in my summary paper on repeat reports.[42]

Thus, families within the population reported for CA/N are largely near or in poverty. What if we look at this from the other direction? Do poor populations generally produce more reports of child maltreatment? The answer is, yes. Community and neighborhood comparisons have shown higher incidences of child maltreatment in areas of high and moderate child poverty compared to areas with low child poverty. A number of studies have shown that maternal age and residence in neighborhoods of poverty strongly predicts substantiated reports of child maltreatment.[43] For instance, Claudia Coulton and associates demonstrated the relationship in a Midwestern urban area. Brett Drake and Shanta Pandey did the same for an entire Midwestern state demonstrating a relationship by neighborhood. Another study based on family surveys showed that child abuse potential was predicted by neighborhood impoverishment and child care burden.[44]

There is a correlation, then, in both directions. Reports of CA/N are received significantly and substantially more often in impoverished neighborhoods and communities, including families whose incomes fall below the official poverty level and others with incomes somewhat above that level. And, when we examine groups of reported families we find high proportions of poor or near poor families. As noted earlier, poverty in a technologically advanced society like ours is a structural variable. When we say someone is poor, we are placing them on the lowest rungs of the income and wealth ladder in comparison to others

---

42   L. Anthony Loman. (2006). *Families Frequently Encountered in Child Protection Services: A Report on Chronic Child Abuse and Neglect.* Institute of Applied Research. Available at: http://www.iarstl.org/papers/FEfamiliesChronicCAN.pdf

43   Here are two examples: Claudia J. Coulton, Jill E. Korbin, Marilyn Su & Julian Chow. (1995). Community level factors and child maltreatment rates. *Child Development, 66,* 1262-1276. Brett Drake & Shanta Pandey. (1996). Understanding the relationship between neighborhood poverty and specific types of child maltreatment. *Child Abuse and Neglect,* 20(11), 1003-1018.

44   Claudia J. Coulton, Jill E. Korbin & Marilyn Su. (1999). Neighborhoods and child maltreatment: A multi-level study. *Child Abuse and Neglect,* 23(11), 1019-1040.

in society. We might take it further and say, they are not just poor, but they are a member of the lowest class, their socioeconomic status. As also explained, this more general ranking takes into account not only income and wealth but other related variables such as level of education and the status of employment. It also sometimes utilizes other characteristics like participation in poverty programs, as in the NIS study.

C. Economic Hardship and Poverty are Sometimes Mistaken for Child Neglect

There is a second sense, however, in which the connection is direct. The explanation in this case is interpretational. This happens when we *label* a set of *behaviors* of a child's impoverished caregiver or circumstances of a poor family as child neglect and sometimes even as child maltreatment. The behaviors or circumstances are usually labeled as child neglect, but they are actually poverty. In this schema poverty does not cause child maltreatment. Rather, it is mistaken for child maltreatment.

Leroy Pelton, of happy memory, was one of the doyens of studies in this area. Pelton began writing about the relationship between class and child maltreatment in 1978. In a 2015 article, he discussed the two approaches mentioned in final section of the previous chapter.[45] As an example of the first, he notes that parental stress is associated with financial needs. Not having enough money to pay for necessities is emotionally difficult.

Pelton noted that poverty and unmet material needs frequently involve safety hazards which parents have difficulty avoiding that is sometimes reported as child neglect.

Like many of the cases described in Chapter 2, the following case clearly illustrates how poverty is sometimes mistaken for child

---

45   Here are some of Pelton's essays: Leroy H. Pelton. (1978). Child abuse and neglect: The myth of classlessness. *American Journal of Orthopsychiatry,* 48, 608–617. Leroy H. Pelton. (1989). For reasons of poverty: A critical analysis of the public child welfare system in the United States. Westport, CT: Praeger. Leroy H. Pelton. (1994). The role of material factors in child abuse and neglect. In Gary B. Melton & Frank D. Barry (Eds.), *Protecting children from abuse and neglect: Foundations for a new national strategy* (pp. 131–181). New York, NY: Guilford Press. Leroy H. Pelton. (2015). The continuing role of material factors in child maltreatment and placement. *Child Abuse and Neglect,* 41 30-39.

maltreatment. This is a case we followed in the District of Columbia. The family had never been reported before. It was a report of unsafe housing.

Case Study 8. On a hot summer day an anonymous report was called into the Child Protection Services (CPS) hotline. The caller was concerned about the welfare of young children, aged 2 and 4, living with their mother in an apartment "in horrible conditions." The reporter described mouse droppings and mold throughout the unit, a nonfunctioning heating and cooling system, and concerns about the presence of lead. The reporter was unaware of any evidence of violence, substance abuse, or mistreatment of the children by a caregiver.

A search of agency records turned up no prior contact with *CPS*—no previous investigations, removals or referrals to *community* services. Two days after the report was received a family assessment (FA) social worker attempted to visit the family, but the mother, who worked part time, was not home, so the worker left a sealed notification letter with the caregiver's mother. (Family assessment is an alternative "family friendly" approach to families that contrasts with adversarial approach utilized in traditional CA/N investigations. It was part of the differential response (DR) program operating in the District of Columbia. Two days later the social worker met and interviewed the four year-old at her preschool. The worker found the child clean, neatly groomed and dressed, without apparent injuries or complaints of harm. When asked about her home, the girl said "me and mommy clean the house…. the mouse pooped all over the house." The girl told the social worker her mother cooks for the two children daily and bathes them nightly. The next day the social worker saw the two-year-old in his daycare center and found no visible signs of abuse or neglect. The worker later checked the immunization histories of the children and found them to be up to date.

Seven days later the social worker met with the mother who showed the worker through the apartment, a publicly subsidized unit, pointing out problems she said she had been complaining about to the property management company. Walking through the apartment the social worker observed mice running through the unit, mouse droppings in every room and on beds, bugs on ceilings and corners of the rooms, a leaking ceiling in the bathroom, a broken refrigerator, two ice chests purchased by the mother to hold perishable food, an air conditioning unit that did not work. The woman told the social worker there had been no heat in the unit the previous winter and that her children suffered from bug bites, asthma and respiratory problems. The family received $468 a month in public assistance, of which 60% was required to be paid to the property management company for the apartment.

The next day, in a meeting initiated by the FA worker, a representative of the agency that had helped the woman find the apartment said she was aware of the condition of the unit and that it was inspected monthly; it had been inspected and approved prior to the woman's taking occupancy. The housing worker said it was the woman's responsibility to "create a paper trail" to document her requests for maintenance repairs; without it the agency could not move the family to a less deplorable apartment. The mother said this is difficult for her; the worker noted that the young mother had experienced "trauma" that included "loss of a child and being threatened with a handgun in the presence of her children while walking to her mom's house at night to seek a warm environment." The worker contacted a community collaborative seeking alternative housing for the family and requested a food voucher from her own agency.

Twenty days after the hotline report, with assistance from a community collaborative, temporary shelter was found in a "hotel," although a roach infestation required the family to move three times over a three-day period, and the family moved out and began staying temporarily "with different family members."

The social worker continued to solicit help from inside and outside her agency but was unable to find suitable housing for the family. The worker attempted to assist the family in dealing with the property management company through an appeal to the DC Superior Court. Since the woman had given the company 30-days' notice to terminate her lease, the court determined that nothing could be done. The worker turned to Legal Aide seeking help.

With assistance from the community collaborative, temporary accommodations were obtained for the family in a motel that also served as a housing shelter. Through a Partnering Together conference the family's case was transferred to the collaborative for case management (for assistance with housing, employment and basic needs) and 54 days after the report was first made the FA referral was closed.

The characteristics of this case are not unusual for families reported for inadequate or unhealthy housing. Those who are not convinced that hundreds of thousands of families face similar situations in the United States might read Matthew Desmond's Evicted, a book that I referenced earlier.[46]

D. How Alleged Victims in All Child Maltreatment Reports came to be approached as Battered Children

Modern Child Protection Services had its origins in the 1960's. The focus was on cases of severe physical abuse, so-called *battered children*, as described by the physician Henry Kemp and his associates. They published initial findings about children observed in emergency rooms and by medical professionals in the Journal of the American Medical Association (JAMA).[47] This contributed to the growing awareness that large numbers of children were at risk of physical abuse. These were cases observed mainly by doctors who tended to understand human conditions in medical terms. I referred to this previously as the *medical model*. As noted, the approach intrinsic to the medical model is individualistic and biological. In the 1960's and later this model and various psychological models were the dominant approaches to understanding child abuse and neglect. For example, here is a quote by Steele and Pollack, from Helfer and Kemp's influential book on child abuse in 1968.[48]

---

46   Matthew Desmond. (2016). Evicted: Poverty and Profit in the American City. New York: Random House.

47   C. Henry Kempe, Frederic Silverman, Brandt Steele, Willian Groegemueller & Henry Silver. 1962. The Battered Child Syndrome. *Journal of the American Medical Association, 181*:17-24.

48   B. F. Steele & C. Pollock. (1968). A psychiatric study of parents who abuse infants and small children. In Ray E. Helfer & C. Henry Kemp (Eds.), *The Battered Child*. Chicago: University of Chicago Press. This quote was taken from the article by Richard J. Gelles on violence toward children discussed below.

"Social, economic, and demographic factors… are somewhat irrelevant to the actual act of child abuse. Unquestionably, social and economic difficulties and disasters put added stress in people's lives and contribute to behavior which might otherwise remain dominant. But such factors must be considered incidental enhancers rather than necessary and sufficient causes."[49]

Granted that the writers were referring to severe physical abuse, the kinds of cases in the "less than one percent of reports" category considered earlier. Nonetheless, this attitude came to dominate thinking about all forms of child abuse and neglect. Social and economic problems are only "incident enhancers." The real problems lay in the psychology and biology of the parent!

Child Protection Services (CPS) programs were established in each U.S. state during the 1960's and 70's. The new laws required a variety of professionals, such as physicians, teachers, law enforcement officials, counselors, and social workers to report suspected child abuse and neglect. They and others professionals became known as "mandated reporters." With the federal Child Abuse Prevention and Treatment Act (CAPTA) of 1974, reporting became mandatory nationwide. Telephone reporting systems for child abuse and neglect were developed. Public listings or registries of CA/N perpetrators were set up with the hope that by tracking them they might be prevented from abusing children again. When abuse or neglect was substantiated, CPS cases were opened to monitor and, in theory, to assist families in the hopes of preventing new incidents of abuse and neglect.

After 1974, child maltreatment became more broadly defined to include the many different categories. Elizabeth Hutchison describes the history clearly at in an article she wrote.[50] She documented the move from reports of battered children to a much wider array of reported threats. The general public was also encouraged to report child abuse and neglect and consequently public awareness and acceptance of CA/N reporting grew. The consequence was a skyrocketing of CA/N reports from a few thousand per year in the late 1960s to several million per year in the 1990's.

---

49   Ibid. Steele and Pollock, page 94.
50   Elizabeth D. Hutchison. (1993). Mandatory Reporting Laws: Child Protective Case Finding Gone Awry? *Social Work 38*, 1, 56-63.

Even by the time of Leroy Pelton's first article on class and CA/N in 1978 and the actual types of CA/N reports received had expanded to include many other categories, including millions of child neglect allegations as well as reports of less severe physical abuse, such as over-severe physical discipline. In his 1978 article, Pelton argued that CA/N was not broadly distributed throughout society. He provided evidence that it was instead related to social class. In his last article in 2015, Pelton went on to address the issue of prospective studies in a section asking whether changes in child maltreatment rates follow changes in material support. He correctly asserted that experimental studies are rare, like the ones reviewed in the next chapter, in which families in different groups are provided with varying levels of extra money or material support and outcomes are tracked.

There are two other issues: parental intentions and the possibility of class bias. Do parents accused of child maltreatment always *intend* to harm their children? Here is a quote from the Pelton article regarding this:

"…injuries due to neglect (which accounts for a far greater percentage of child abuse and neglect incidents than does abuse) are largely unintentional. They can be viewed as a subset of a far larger realm of unintentional injuries, or accidents. There is much evidence that heightened risk of severe accidental injury to children, like child abuse and neglect, is strongly related to low socioeconomic status… The direct way in which the material deficits of poverty may lead to child harm with attribution of neglect to parents may also lead to it without such attribution. Because of our society's intense focus on child abuse beginning in the 1960s, it is arguable that while many incidents of severe injury might have once been mistakenly attributed to mere accident, there may now be an over-attribution of such incidents to parental fault. Moreover, even beyond that, there has always been an inclination within the child welfare system to call a lack of resources, such as adequate housing, child neglect; that is, to confuse poverty itself with neglect."[51]

---

51   Leroy H. Pelton. (2015). The continuing role of material factors in child maltreatment and placement. *Child Abuse and Neglect*, 41 30-39.

As you look at examples in this book, ask yourself this question again. Did the parents *intend* to harm their children? Pelton emphasizes neglect, but in our opinion a large portion of less severe child abuse can also be characterized as unintentional. In the following example, the arm bruises observed by the teacher were not intentionally inflicted by his mother. We grant that she needed instruction in other non-physical ways of controlling and disciplining her boys, but was substantiation of child abuse and entry of the mother's name into the state registry of child abusers the best method? This was an urban mother-only family. In this case the mother was employed. We were unable to review the financial circumstances of the family, although it can be assumed that like most mother-only families she was at best in a *near poverty* situation.

A teacher reported that a boy in her class had bruises on his arms that he said came from getting a paddling by his mother. He was about seven years old. Physical punishment leaving bruises, scrapes or red marks was considered extreme and potentially child abuse. The investigator went to the home and interviewed the single mother, who admitted that she had indeed spanked the boy. She said she kept the sharp knives on top the refrigerator because she did not trust her son to leave them alone, as he was somewhat hyperactive. He had convinced his younger brother to have a 'sword fight' and had climbed up on the cabinet and retrieved two knives. His mother caught them doing this and said that she had 'lost it.' She spanked the older boy with a paddle that she kept in the house and he had put his arms behind him to protect himself and thus was bruised. The investigator thought this was too minor to substantiate but her supervisor told her that this was definitely physical abuse and she had to issue a formal finding of abuse. Child abuse was substantiated, and a case was opened.

Regarding child abuse, a well-known older study by Richard Gelles on *Poverty and Violence toward Children* was based on interviews of parents in two national surveys.[52] As we have noted, the prevailing idea up to that time (1960-90) was that child abuse and neglect was present across all social classes. The common understanding was that CA/N was to be explained psychologically and medically. The economic situation

---

52   Richard J. Gelles. (1992). Poverty and Violence toward Children. *American Behavioral Scientist*, 35, 3, 258,274.

of families, their environments and social context were regarded as of little consequence. Gelles' studies strongly supported the causal effect of economic deprivation and the consequent stress in families on violence toward children.

Some who do not accept this idea have offered another explanation of the correlation between poverty and child maltreatment reporting: class bias. It is not uncommon to hear the suggestion that child abuse and neglect is endemic in all social classes and at all income levels, as the quote above from Steele and Pollack asserted. The reason why poverty seems to be associated with CA/N, these commentators say, is simply that poor people are reported more often. The idea is that poor parents and children are more likely to come into contact with professionals, such as social workers, welfare workers, law enforcement, and many others, mandated reporters who are required to make reports when they encounter possible CA/N. Not only that, it is asserted that middle- and upper-class professionals are biased toward poor parents, and are more likely to attribute negligence and laziness and physical abusiveness to them. Thus, middle- and upper-class CA/N is ignored but it is usually reported when observed among poor people. There are many studies demonstrating that this is incorrect. While it is not illogical, there is no systematic evidence that such bias exists at a level sufficient to account for the level of income disparity between child welfare populations and the general population of children and families. The difference is more likely the result of factors associated with low income. There are many studies documenting this.[53] A recent one by Hyunil Kim, Brett Drake and Melissa Johnson-Reid is particularly worth reading. They studied professional reporting at the individual level in four states and at the county level nationwide. They found that higher levels of poverty were not associated with increases in reports by professionals.[54]

Another author who has written extensively on poverty and CA/N is Duncan Lindsey. A wonderful older book he wrote that influenced

---

53   Here are two studies. Brett Drake & Susan Zuravin. (1998). Bias in child maltreatment reporting: Revisiting the myth of classlessness. *American Journal of Orthopsychiatry, 68,* 2, 295-304. Melissa Jonson-Reed, Brett Drake & Patricia L. Kohl. (2009). Is the overrepresentation of the poor in child welfare caseloads due to bias or needs? *Children and Youth Services Review, 31,* 422-427.

54   Hyunil Kim, Brett Drake & Melissa Jonson-Reid. (2018). An examination of class-based visibility bias in national child maltreatment reporting. *Children and Youth Services Review, 85,* 165-173. The work of Jonson-Read and Drake and their students concerning the relation of poverty and CA/N is also informative.

my thinking is *The Welfare of Children*.[55] It is still worth reading. Lindsey asserts and offers evidence that the fundamental problem that underlies most cases encountered by child protection agencies is child and family poverty. He presents evidence showing the ineffectiveness of social casework in producing changes in families. The reason is not so much that social work with families is a waste of time. Rather the problem is the restrictive ideology that traditionally surrounded social work with families accused of child maltreatment. Lindsey called it the *residual approach*. Under this way of thinking, only the most severe cases are given services while less severe cases are provided minimal or no assistance other than monitoring. In addition, the severe cases that do receive services are provided with only enough assistance to bring them back to a level of *minimally acceptable functioning*. Then the case is closed. Some of the intensive services described in the next chapter were delivered in programs that specifically rejected the residual approach to child welfare. Lindsey advocated for basic legislative and social changes that would reduce child poverty and income inequality. We agree that this is the ultimate solution. Primary poverty prevention programs will alleviate a large portion of child abuse and neglect in the US.

Lindsey was the principal editor of a major journal in this field, *Children and Youth Services Review*, which has published many articles over the years concerning poverty and child welfare. Readers who want to educate themselves further beyond the few tastes of opinion and research presented so far might turn to Volume 72 of that journal, published in 2017, which was devoted completely to these topics. It was titled, *Economic Causes and Consequences of Child Maltreatment*. It consisted of 15 research articles from a variety of perspectives. We briefly review one of those in the next section.[56]

Here are the titles of the articles in this volume: Child welfare involvement and contexts of poverty: 1. The role of parental adversities, social networks, and social services. 2. Economic predictors of child maltreatment in an Australian population-based birth cohort. 3. The influence of concrete support on child welfare program engagement,

---

55   Duncan Lindsey. (1994). *The Welfare of Children*. New York: Oxford University Press.
56   Here is the web access address: https://www.sciencedirect.com/journal/children-and-youth-services-review/vol/72/suppl/C

progress, and recurrence. 4. Out-of-home placement and regional variations in poverty and health and social services spending: A multilevel analysis. 5. Intersections of individual and neighborhood disadvantage: Implications for child maltreatment. 6. Pathways of risk and resilience between neighborhood socioeconomic conditions and parenting. 7. Money matters: Does the minimum wage affect child maltreatment rates? 8. The Great Recession and risk for child abuse and neglect. 9. The effect of lowering welfare payment ceilings on children's risk of out-of-home placement. 10. The impact of income on reunification among families with children in out-of-home care. 11. Making parents pay: The unintended consequences of charging parents for foster care. 12. The effect of monthly stipend on the placement instability of youths in out-of-home care. 13. The potential educational benefits of extending foster care to young adults: Findings from a natural experiment. 14. Employment outcomes of young parents who age out of foster care. 15. Adverse childhood experiences and life opportunities: Shifting the narrative.

Chapter 4

Six Studies in Five States

In this chapter I deemphasize questions of *how* poverty and material needs are related to child and family welfare. Instead, six studies that address the *whether* question are considered. Five of these are large scale field experiments: give families in the experimental group money or help them meet their material needs but provide less or none to control/comparison group. Then observe what happens.

Before looking at these, we might look at a couple of recent prospective studies by others. In a Wisconsin study in 2013, Cancian, Yang and Slack studied slightly over 13,000 Cash Welfare (TANF) families who were randomly assigned to one of two nearly equal-sized groups.[57] In the experimental group (50.4%), families were able to keep their entire child support payments. In the second, the control group (49.6%), families were permitted to keep only a part. As we have noted, random assignment creates virtually equivalent groups in all important ways. In experiments, the ideal is then to do something to one group and something else (or nothing) to the other group and then observe the groups for outcomes of interest. If random assignment is carried out correctly, the only important difference (statistically) between the two groups is what is subsequently done to the families or individuals. All child support money ($200) was passed through to the experimental families while partial child support money ($50) was passed through to control group families. However, experimental families only received an average of $101 more than control families in the first two years. One of the outcomes of interest was subsequent accepted reports of

---

57   Maria Cancian, Mi-Youn Yang & Kristen Shook Slack. (2013). The effect of additional child support income on the risk of child maltreatment. *Social Service Review, 87,* 417–437. As noted earlier, TANF refers to Temporary Assistance for Needy Families, the highly restrictive program, enacted under Bill Clinton, which replaced the older and more generous AFDC program that provided modest money to impoverished families with children.

child abuse and neglect. The researchers found that the increased income was associated with a later reduction in child abuse and neglect reports that were accepted and investigated. The question of what specifically occurred to make this happen when more money came into families was not answered. The value of experiments of this kind is that differences observed have to be attributed to the treatment, that is, what was done to the experimental group but not done to the control group. The statistical difference between the groups was the disparity in incomes: experimental families got more than control families. More money reduced later screened-in maltreatment reports. Only about one in every five families experienced a new report, and among these, experimental families received an estimated 2% fewer reports. This is not a large reduction but it was statistically significant, that is, very unlikely to have been due to chance factors. This is a modest difference but then the difference in support provided was also modest.

A second experiment is worth reporting in this regard. It is one of the articles in the aforementioned 2017 *Children and Youth Services Review* volume devoted to poverty and child maltreatment. It was conducted by Rostad, McGill-Rogers and Chaffin.[58] The program they studied involved families with open child welfare cases who were receiving home-based services. Most were cases substantiated for child neglect. Up to $600 could be spent per family to help with various needs, such as utility payments, food, clothing or transportation. The needs were real since eight of every ten of these families were living in poverty—a typical population of families being served under a CPS program. This group, however, was composed of frequently encountered families with multiple previous reports, which as we have noted are the poorest of the poor. The study design was quasi-experimental because the groups of families that were to be treated differently could not be created through random assignment. Instead, demographic characteristics were used to create matched groups.[59] The study found that families with increased material support were more engaged and more satisfied and, most importantly, the odds of a new

---

58   Whitney L. Rostad, Tia McGill Rogers & Mark J. Chaffin. (2017). The Influence of Concrete Support on Child Welfare Program Engagement, Progress, and Recurrence. *Children and Youth Services Review, 72*, 26-33.

59   The method utilized *was propensity score matching.* If you want to read about this method look up the informative Wikipedia article on propensity score matching.

report of CA/N within one year were reduced by 11%. The authors had also hypothesized that parental stress would be reduced, but no differences were found for this outcome.

Why do studies utilize reductions in new accepted reports of child maltreatment as a measure of improved child safety and welfare? The absence of new reports on previously reported families is an indirect measure. It tells us that the behavior of caregivers toward their children did not deteriorate to an extent that is likely to result in them being reported for child abuse or neglect. On the other hand, it is a consistent and available measure because records of reports are stored and maintained in large agency databases, and because, other things being equal, large groups of families reported for CA/N have the same probability of being re-reported. We should note that the measure we utilize is accepted report, whether or not the report was later confirmed or disconfirmed. In the traditional system, two-thirds or more of accepted reports go unsubstantiated. Yet the evidence is strong that the proper measure of risk (as defined in probability terms) is reports alone, whether confirmed or not. I analyzed this extensively in the previously cited study of *Frequently Encountered Families*.[60]

A. Two Title IV-E Waiver Experiments

Title IV-E of the Social Security Act provides states and tribes with funding to assist with the costs of foster care maintenance for eligible children; administrative expenses to manage the program; and training for staff, foster parents, and certain private agency staff. Eligibility varies somewhat from state to state but generally the families and children served are either in or near official poverty levels. States must provide a percentage match to the federal dollars. In the present studies the federal contribution amounted to around two-thirds of the total foster care cost. Thus, for every $100 spent to provide foster care for a qualifying child the states received $60-70 in compensation. In the projects considered here, Mississippi and Indiana were granted waivers from the standard IV-E spending rules. The states were permitted to spend monies more broadly and flexibly. These are examples of what

---

60   L. Anthony Loman. (2006). *Families Frequently Encountered in Child Protection Services:* A Report on Chronic Child Abuse and Neglect. Institute of Applied Research. Available at: http://www.iarstl. org/papers/FEfamiliesChronicCAN.pdf

we earlier referred to as *intensive services.* Funds that traditionally could only be spent to pay for foster care could now be used to address family needs of various kinds. There was also greater *flexibility* in utilizing available funds, including addressing the material needs of involved families. In both states, the waiver programs included children who had been removed from their families and placed in out-of-home care as well as children who were in danger of being removed but were permitted to remain in their homes. For the former group of children, a primary goal was shortening the length of time that the child remained in foster care. For the latter, it was preventing removal.

As noted, the children in the studies represented the most extreme side of the child protection/child welfare spectrum, very high-risk cases. Dangers to their ongoing safety and welfare were determined to be high enough to warrant their removal from their homes.

Study 1: The Mississippi Title IV-E Waiver Experiment

This study took place during a 42-month period from April 2001 through September 2004 in six Mississippi counties.[61] To get a sense of the population of families included in the study, Mississippi was ranked first in child poverty among the 50 states in 2000, first in the percent of families in poverty, first in the number of households headed by single women, and 47th in median household income.

Initially families and children in existing Title IV-E eligible cases were identified and submitted to a random assignment program on portable computers we supplied to the six local offices. New cases continued to be assigned during subsequent months. Experimental children and their families were eligible for intensive services paid for with IV-E funds; control cases were not. By the time of the final analysis, 777 experimental children in 346 families and 772 control children in 321 families were available for analysis. Experimental and Control groups were similar. No statistically significant differences were found in the following demographic or case characteristics (Table 4.1).

61　Gary L. Siegel & L. Anthony Loman. (2005). *State of Mississippi Title IV-E Child Welfare Waiver Demonstration Project. Institute of Applied Research.* Available at: https://www.iarstl.org/papers/ MSIVEFinalReport.pdf

Table 4.1. Characteristics of Experimental and Control Children and Families					
Children	Experimental (n=777)	Control (n=772)	Families	Experimental (n=346)	Control (n=321)
Risk Level			No. of Children		
High	61.1%	60.0%	One	35.1%	37.6%
Medium	35.6%	37.6%	Two	21.8%	25.9%
Low	2.4.%	2.5%	Three or more	43.1%	36.5%
Gender			Race		
Male	47.2%	50.3%	White	51.9%	45.0%
Female	52.8%	49.7%	Black	34.5%	44.1%
Race			Mixed	9.3%	8.4%
White	48.5%	42.6%	Household		
Black	38.5%	44.0%	Female Present	92.2%	91.9%
Asian	.2%	.1%	Male Present	44.9%	42.2%
Unindicated	12.8%	13.1%	Female & Male Present	39.1%	37.2%

Nearly all the children were rated by CPS investigators as high or medium risk at the time of entry into the random assignment program. This is a confirmation that this study concerned CPS cases from the more dangerous end of the child safety spectrum. Differences in racial designations between children and families illustrate inaccuracies and inconsistencies in such designations in the state's data system, something we found many times in other states. A mother was present in the large majority of families but only about four in ten were two-parent. About six in every ten families involved child neglect, and in many of those cases the neglect was actually family poverty along the lines of the case examples presented earlier.

Services. Figure 4.1 shows the differences in material services of various kinds during the months the families and their children were on the waiver.

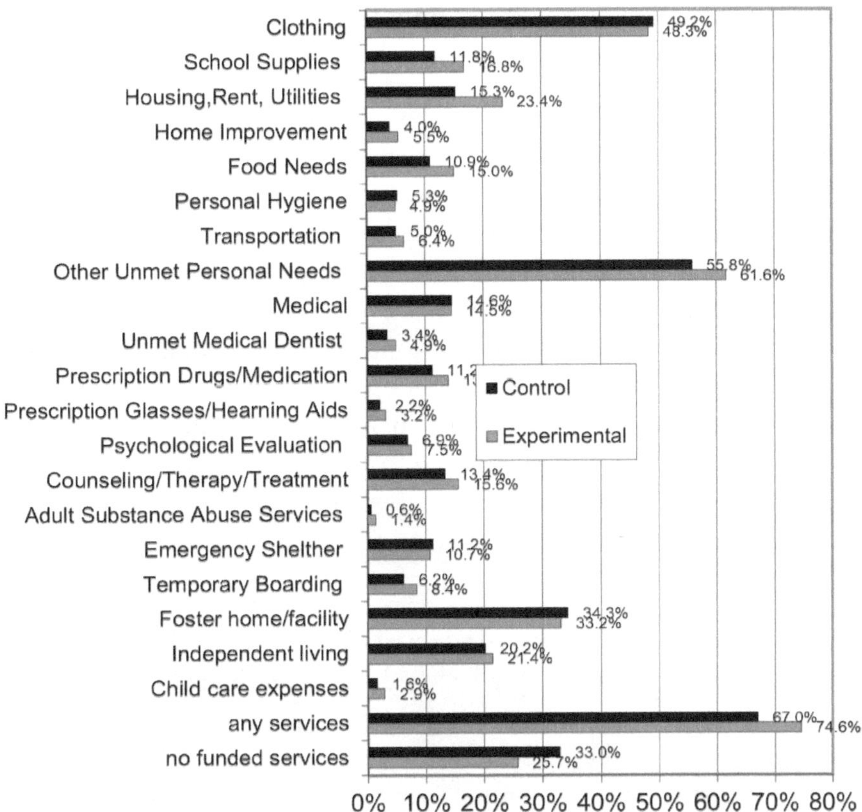

Figure 4.1. Services Provided During the Mississippi Waiver

The service increases were modest overall. Total funded services increased for experimental families (Experimental (E): 75%; Control (C): 67%). Here are some examples: Money for housing, rent and utilities (E: 23%; C: 15%); Food needs (E: 15%; C: 11%); Prescription drugs and medications (E: 14%; C: 11%); Other personal needs (E: 62%; C: 56%); School supplies (E: 17%; C: 12%). Looking across all services received, experimental families and children received an average of 3.2 different services compared to 2.8 for control families.

Outcomes. We examined whether these increases in mainly material services had any positive effects. We found that subsequent new child maltreatment reports occurred in 19.7% of control cases compared to 14.5% of Experimental cases. This difference was substantial considering the short time frames involved (less than two years for most cases) and was statistically significant (p = .004).

When considering specific types of maltreatment, a statistically significant difference was found in new reports of physical abuse: 3.7 percent of experimental children had new incident reports of physical abuse compared with 6.0% of control children (p=.02). Differences between the two groups in new reports of neglect or sexual abuse were not significant, although the differences were in the hypothesized direction: 12.4% of experimental children had new neglect reports compared to 14.6% of control children; and 2.4% of experimental children had new reports of sexual maltreatment compared to 3.0% of control children. The pattern seen in Figure 4.2 of more reports for control children was found for both pre-existing cases and new cases. It was also found for cases that had closed prior to the end of data collection and those that remained open.

A survival analysis was conducted that considered variations in time after each target case had closed. This method considers both *whether* new reports occur and *how long it was* before they occurred. This time period is referred to as *survival time,* that is, how long the family "survives" until a terminal event occurs. In this case the event was a new accepted report of child maltreatment.[62] Control children experienced new reports sooner. Thus, more reports were recorded for this group during the follow-up period. The experimental-control differences are shown in Figure 4.2 and were statistically significant (p = .03).

---

62   This was a simple life-table analysis. It involved no statistical controls. The analysis is described and shown graphically in the original report (Siegel and Loman, ibid., pages 64-65). Survival analysis as applied to the recurrence of reports of child abuse and neglect is concerned with the period of time until a new report occurs. In an experimental study, separate life tables can be constructed for the experimental and control groups. Then the survival times of cases in the experimental group can be compared to those in the control group to see if, as a whole, they are different. If the overall difference is great enough to be unlikely to have occurred by chance, we can assert that the experiment was a success.

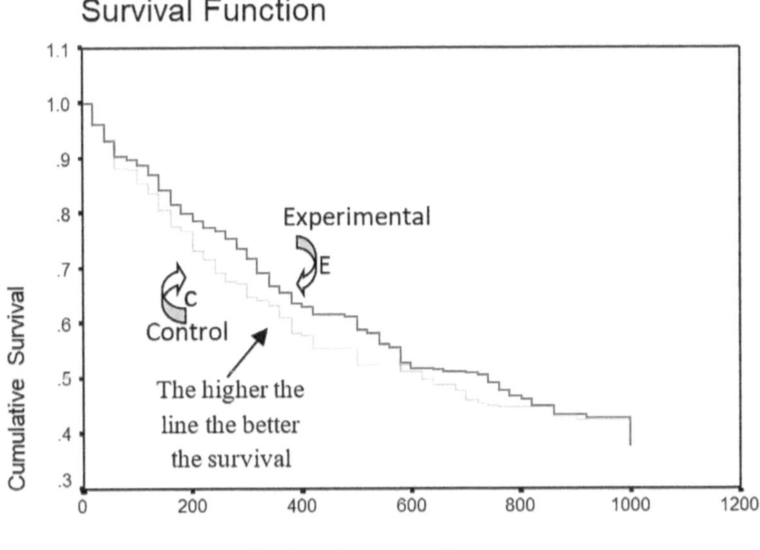

Figure 4.2. Survival of Experimental and Control Families Until A New Child Maltreatment Report (20-day intervals)

Perhaps most importantly, we were able to show that the greatest differences occurred for children *who received services.* The reduction in new reports of child maltreatment in such cases amounted to 5.6% (E: 15.8%; C: 21.4%; p = .04). The increase in material services had positive effects on families.

In addition, under the waiver program children who remained with their parents were less likely to be removed (9.1%) than similar control children (14.1%). Again, and most importantly, the effects were powerful in families that received services. Among those families 33.1% of children were later removed compared to 57.2% in control families. This also was shown to be a real difference when variations in time were considered. A survival analysis confirmed that control children experienced out-of-home placement more often and *sooner* than experimental children (p = .025)

The Mississippi IV-E experiment demonstrated that spending money on poor families improved the subsequent welfare and safety of the children. Intensive services to such families enhanced their stability and reduced the likelihood that children would later be taken into state custody.

Study 2: The Indiana Title IV-E Waiver Experiment

We conducted a similar intensive and flexible services experimental study in Indiana over a five-year period (2005-2010).[63] Because the state would not permit random assignment to experimental and control groups, a child-matching design was developed.[64] The object was not to produce matched pairs for analytic purposes but to produce matched groups for final group comparisons. The numbers eventually assigned were exceptionally large and by the conclusion of the study there 9,475 experimental (waiver) children in closed cases and 9,358 similar control children available for comparison.

As a part of the waiver program design, Indiana was permitted to assign up to half of children to the program who were not *eligible* for Title IV-E services. This was permitted so long as the state maintained cost-neutrality, that is, so long as no greater expenditures took place than would have taken place under the traditional IV-E program. Characteristics of waiver and control children can be seen in Table 4.2.

---

63   L. Anthony Loman, Christine Shannon Filonow & Gary L. Siegel. (2011). *Indiana IV-E Child Welfare Waiver Extension: Final Evaluation Report.* Institute of Applied Research. Available at: https://www.iarstl.org/papers/Indiana%20IV-E%20Final%20Evaluation%20Report-2011.pdf

64   Children assigned to the waiver were pair-matched on a monthly basis with children not assigned. 12 weighted characteristics were utilized in producing summated scores for each newly assigned waiver child and for all non-waiver children. Weighting: 1. IV-E eligibility (100); 2. Case Type, including service (voluntary, court request, court ordered), service (adoption, AG, DOC, IL), SRA, IA, CHINS, and Delinquent (64); 3. Special Needs: psychological, medical, developmental disabilities and disabilities (64); 4. Case Begin Date (50); 5. Placement / Removal status (36); 6. Case County (32); 7. Age (16); 8. Physical Abuse (12); 9. Sexual Abuse (12); 10. Neglect (8); 11. Gender (8); 12. Number of Caregivers (8).

Table 4.2 Characteristics of Indiana Experiment and Control Children					
	Experimental	Control		Experimental	**Control**
Title IV-E Eligible	47.9%	49.3%	*Case Type at Assignment*		
Title IV-E Not Eligible	52.1%	50.7%	Child in Need of Services	54.7%	61.5%
Male	53.9%	53.7%	Informal Adjustment	21.5%	16.2%
Female	46.1%	46.3%	Service Referral	3.1%	2.2%
Mean Age (all children)	8.6 yrs.	8.8 yrs.	Service	8.5%	6.8%
Mean Age CPS children	7.7 yrs.	7.7 yrs.	Juvenile Delinquent	12.2%	13.1%
Mean Age of Delinquents	15.48	15.57	*Placement History*		
Household Characteristics			Placed at waiver assignment	36.6%	40.4%
Mean household size	5.2	5.1	Placed prior to waiver assign.	54.3%	66.8%
Two or more adult caregivers	64.4%	63.7%	2 or more prior removals	10.3%	9.4%
One adult caregiver	35.5%	36.1%	*Placed in:*		
Single mother households	30.6%	30.1%	Foster care	65.6%	70.4%
Special Needs			Relative care	29.4%	20.0%
Psychological Problems	10.5%	11.5%	Institutional care	25.3%	32.0%
Medical Conditions	0.3%	0.3%	Correctional facilities	4.2%	6.4%
MR/DD	4.8%	5.2%	Other facilities/ settings	17.8%	13.4%
Physical Disabilities	2.9%	2.8%	One type of facility	59.8%	61.1%

Any Special Need	14.7%	15.7%	Two or more types of facilities	40.1%	38.8%
Multiple Conditions	3.3%	3.4%			

The two groups were highly similar on a variety of characteristics suggesting that the matching procedures were accurate and effective. Differences can be seen in some initial case types but these types shifted and changed in the period following case opening. As can be seen, this study included delinquent youths as well as children in CPS cases. Delinquents were, of course, older as a group. The placement statistics illustrate the high-risk nature of most of the cases.

Services. Services to families and children expanded significantly and substantially for many types. Workers in experimental cases were more likely to report that families had received services to prevent placement (89.3%) than workers in control cases (75.0%) (p < .0001). They were also more likely to report that families had received services in the home after reunification took place (76.5% versus 50.7%, p < .0001).

Service categories with the strongest differences were those that addressed financial insecurity or family integrity. For example, 42.7% of experimental families received aid for household needs as compared with 14.0% of control families. Regarding more basic and individual needs the difference was 30.6% for experimentals versus 16.2% for controls. Experimental families in 38.8% of cases had a homemaker visit and help them compared to 26.6% of control families. The full panoply of service differences can be examined in the original report noted above.

Families were also surveyed. While response rates were substantially lower among families in comparison to workers, family responses were consistent with those of workers indicating substantial increases in services of various kinds, including material services and community-based referrals. Experimental families were more likely to indicate that services received were the kind they really needed and were enough to help.

Looking at state financial records, we found that overall spending on services averaged $2,472 per experimental child compared to $708 per control child. Among control children 26.7% received a service purchased by the state compared to 64.3% of experimental children.

Outcomes. Outcomes were also tracked. The major goals of the demonstration were: 1) preventing/reducing out-of-home placements; 2) reducing lengths of stay in out-of-home care; 3) decreasing the incidence and recurrence of child maltreatment; and 4) enhancing child and family well-being.

Beginning at the time of assignment and tracking forward until the end of the case (or the end of current data collection), 15.7% of experimental children had subsequently been removed and placed in out-of-home care compared to 18.0% of control children, a difference that was statistically significant (p = .003). Time in out-of-home placement was reduced for waiver children (E: 314 days, C: 427 days; p < .001).

Among closed CPS cases substantially more experimental children (n = 4,076) were reunified with their families (E: 63.5%, C: 46.9%; p < .001) whereas more control children (n = 4,177) were not reunified but were adopted into other families (E: 14.2%, C: 30.1%; p < .001). In addition, more experimental children were placed in guardianship (E: 10.6%, C: 8.2%; p < .001). Regarding reunification with family, similar results occurred among delinquents (315 experimental cases with 75.2% reunification, 439 control cases with 68.3% reunification (p = .02).

As noted, experimental families were more likely to report that the kinds of assistance received were what they needed and enough to really help. Relief of these conditions in families generally has positive effects on the relationships of family members and in turn on child development. We found that reported school performance improved among experimental children (p = .037). Waiver families more often reported that their children were much or somewhat better off because of the experience (E: 75.8%, C: 68.4%; p = .017) and similarly that their families were much or somewhat better off (E: 74.5%, C: 66.1%; p = .027).

Conclusions Regarding Title IV-E Waiver Studies. The Indiana and Mississippi experiments concerned the highest risk families and children in the CPS system. They each illustrate the benefits of increased spending on financially related services and addressing material needs. The welfare and safety of children were enhanced in each study. Subsequent reports of child maltreatment decreased significantly in frequency in both projects. The need for removal and placement of children dropped significantly. Time that children had to remain in foster or residential care decreased as well. There were indications of greater family satisfaction with services, improvements in family life, and improvement in school performance of children. Next we turn to two other studies within the CPS system.

B. Studies 3 and 4: Differential Response Projects in Minnesota and Ohio

We conducted two prospective experimental studies in Minnesota and Ohio that addressed financial hardship of families. In each family, child welfare and child safety improved.[65]

The Minnesota study began in 2001 and ran through 2005.[66] It involved over 5,000 families reported to Child Protection Services (CPS) in 20 Minnesota counties. However, the experiment was limited to 14 counties that agreed to random assignment of control cases. For this analysis, 3,861 families were considered: 2,605 experimental families and 1,256 control families. Families were assigned randomly but a weighting was used to keep control numbers to approximately half the size of experimental.[67] Because we were doing other studies in Minnesota, we continued to receive data on study families. The following analysis is based on data from 1999 through 2010.

---

65   Long-term analysis of the Minnesota DR project: L. Anthony Loman & Gary L. Siegel. (2012). Effects of anti-poverty services under the differential response approach to child welfare. *Children and Youth Services Review, 34*, 1659–1666. Five-year follow-up of the Ohio DR project: L. Anthony Loman & Gary L. Siegel. (2015). Effects of approach and services under differential response on long term child safety and welfare. Child Abuse and Neglect, 39, 86-97. Available at: https://www.sciencedirect.com/science/article/pii/S0145213414002099

66   The original final report: L. Anthony Loman and Gary L. Siegel. (2004). *Minnesota Alternative Response Evaluation: Final Report.* Research. Available at: https://www.iarstl.org/papers/ARFinalEvaluationReport.pdf There was also a two-year follow-up report: Gary L. Siegel and L. Anthony Loman. (2006). Institute of Applied Research. Available at: https://www.iarstl.org/papers/FinalMNFARReport.pdf

67   This was necessary to ensure that the 14 participating counties assigned sufficient numbers of children to receive family assessments in order to collect all foundation monies available. Counties received a set amount for each child so assigned. The funds received could be spent on any currently active family assessment case.

The Ohio study began in 2008 and ran through 2013 in 10 Ohio counties.[68] Over 4,600 families were involved and tracked. Again, random assignment was utilized with 2,383 families assigned to the experimental group and 2,247 in the control group.

Both studies involved a new approach in CPS that has come to be called Differential Response (DR). This approach was mentioned in Chapter 3 in the description of the case in the District of Columbia (Case Study 8). The approach excluded families accused of severe physical abuse and neglect or any allegations of sexual abuse. Thus, compared to the two IV-E studies reviewed, these experiments were focused on lower risk cases, usually involving families accused of child neglect of various kinds and less severe physical abuse, such as oversevere discipline.

Under the traditional CPS approach, *all* families with accepted reports alleging child maltreatment were subjected to a forensic and adversarial investigation. The term *adversarial* refers to investigatory behavior similar to that of law enforcement with the objective of determining whether the allegations of the report (or any other maltreatment) really occurred. The families assigned to the control group received this kind of traditional investigation. Investigations were concluded by either substantiating maltreatment or not. Substantiated investigations led to opening and maintaining CPS cases on these families. By contrast, the experimental families were *not investigated.* Instead, they received a non-adversarial *family assessment (FA),* which included a full child-safety assessment but then focused on broader family needs. In some instances, ongoing cases were opened on these families as well, especially if initial assessments of child safety and family needs led to concerns about the welfare and safety of the children. Please refer to the online reports if you want greater details about DR. However, there was another dimension to the experimental treatment in these studies. In each state a private foundation provided extra funding for services to *experimental cases only.* The differential

---

68   The original final report: L. Anthony Loman, Christine Shannon Filonow & Gary L. Siegel. (2010). *Ohio Alternative Response Evaluation: Final Report.* Institute of Applied Research. Available at: https://www.iarstl.org/papers/OhioAREvaluation.pdf . The extended follow-up report: L. Anthony Loman & Gary L. Siegel. (2014). *Ohio Alternative Response Evaluation Extension: Final Report.* Institute of Applied Research. Available at: https://www.iarstl.org/papers/OhioARFinalExtensionReportFINAL.pdf

response approach provided *flexibility and family involvement* in decision-making regarding service needs. The additional funding permitted more intensive services. In this way the approach in these two experiments resembled the approach utilized in the IV-E studies.[69]

Table 4.3. Select Demographic and Cases Characteristics of Study Groups		Minnesota		Ohio	
Experimental (E) – Control (C)		E	C	E	C
Number		2605	1256	2383	2247
Family Characteristics					
Race	Caucasian	71.4%	69.8%	62.2%	63.5%
	African American	17.3%	16.2%	24.9%	24.7%
	Native American	3.3%	3.9%		
	Other or Unknown	8.0%	11.1%	12.4%	11.7%
Persons	Mean number of adults	2.2	2.3	1.72	1.72
	Mean number of children	2.5	2.5	2.01	2.04
Initial Allegations	Neglect	58.1%	58.1%	53.0%	53.9%
	Physical Abuse	42.2%	42.3%	44.1%	44.0%

Services. The additional funding led to higher levels of services for experimental families. The differences are illustrated in Table 4.4, which shows workers' reports of services provided to experimental and control families. The data for these table came from case-specific sample surveys of workers responsible for cases. Like surveys described for the IV-E studies, response rates of workers were high (greater than 85%), with lack of response attributable to worker turnover and worker leave.

As can be seen in Table 4.4, experimental families received more help in nearly every service area but much more in material services of various kinds, such as food and basic household needs (furniture, appliance, clothing, etc.). Also, families were provided cash for rent, childcare, respite care as well as other kinds of financial assistance. The differences in some categories were substantial and in many were statistically significant.

---

69   Minnesota: L. Anthony Loman & Gary L. Siegel. (2012). Effects of anti-poverty services under the differential response approach to child welfare. *Children and Youth Services Review, 34*, 1659–1666. Ohio: L. Anthony Loman & Gary L. Siegel. (2015). Effects of approach and services under differential response on long term child safety and welfare. *Child Abuse and Neglect, 39*, 86-97.

Many of these were services directed toward problems of financial hardship. The FA approach with its emphasis on the underlying needs of families helped FA workers to discover such problems more often than traditional investigators.

FA workers also had more flexibility to address needs that were much more rarely addressed under the traditional *residual approach.* This is not at all surprising. Workers were confronted with families generally ranging in income from extreme poverty to near official poverty levels. They had the means to help, so they helped. Analyses showed that the more the need of the family, the more likely services were provided.

Table 4.4. Worker Reports of Services Provided to Families in the Minnesota and Ohio Alternative Response Studies (Case Review Samples)						
	Minnesota			Ohio		
Service Categories	Control	Experimental	Probability	Control	Experimental	Probability
Help with rent/house payments	2.4%	11.0%	<= .001	3.5%	9.3%	< .05
Housing services	3.9%	9.5%	< .05	3.9%	7.2%	< .10
Help with basic home needs	2.9%	16.1%	<= .001	6.1%	20.3%	<= .001
Emergency food	0.0%	9.9%	<= .001	1.7%	6.8%	< .05
Assistance with transportation	1.9%	8.8%	<= .001	3.9%	7.6%	
TANF, SSI or food stamps	2.9%	7.3%	< .05	2.6%	6.8%	< .05
Medical or dental care	8.2%	9.5%		2.2%	5.9%	< .05
Assistance with employment	1.9%	5.5%	< .05	2.2%	3.8%	

Vocational/skill training	0.5%	4.8%	< .05	0.9%	1.3%	
Educational services	5.3%	7.7%		0.9%	2.5%	
Legal services	4.8%	6.6%		5.2%	4.7%	
Childcare/ daycare services	5.3%	12.8%	< .05	2.6%	8.9%	<= .001
Homemaker/ home management	1.4%	5.8%	< .05	1.7%	2.1%	
Respite care/ crisis nursery	3.9%	7.3%		1.3%	1.7%	
Emergency shelter	1.9%	2.6%		2.2%	2.1%	
Parenting classes	11.6%	18.3%	< .05	4.8%	6.4%	
Marital/ family/group counseling	14.5%	18.6%		4.4%	9.3%	< .05
Individual counseling	15.5%	24.2%	< .05	16.2%	18.6%	
Mental health/ psychiatric services	10.1%	15.3%		9.2%	10.6%	
Drug abuse treatment	6.3%	2.9%		5.2%	1.7%	< .05
Alcohol abuse treatment	4.8%	4.0%		2.2%	3.0%	
Domestic violence services	9.7%	9.5%		4.8%	2.5%	
Assistance from support groups	4.3%	6.6%		1.3%	3.0%	
Disability services	1.9%	2.2%		0.4%	0.8%	
Recreational services	1.4%	5.9%	< .05	0.9%	2.1%	

Family preservation services	3.9%	4.8%		2.6%	1.7%	
Total Families	227	220		207	273	

Outcomes. Did these differences in financial and material aid make a difference in long-term outcomes for families? One important outcome was the percentage of families in the experimental group that were the subject of later reports of child maltreatment. Random assignment made for great similarity between the two groups, and other things being equal, we would expect to see families re-reported at about the same rate. However, this is not what happened. Subsequent child maltreatment reports and investigations occurred significantly *less often* for experimental families. Analysis showed that the risk of new child abuse and neglect investigations in Minnesota was *28% greater for control families.*[70] We also looked at subsequent removals and out-of-home placements of children, which was also significantly lower among experimental families. Subsequent analysis of the data through 2010, some five years after the original follow-up study showed similar results for the full samples of families.[71] However, in that analysis we were able to show that material services to both low-risk and high-risk families were effective in reducing later child maltreatment reports and subsequent child removals.[72]

Here is an example chart from the Ohio study (Figure 4.3). The lines in the chart show the cumulative survival rates, where survival indicates the length of time until a new child maltreatment report was received (the hazard referenced in the chart title). The higher the line the better the survival rate. [73]

---

70   This analysis comes from the MN Follow-up report. Gary L. Siegel and L. Anthony Loman. (2006). *Extended Follow-up Study of Minnesota's Family Assessment Response: Final Report.* Institute of Applied Research, pages 30-1. Available at: https://www.iarstl.org/papers/FinalMNFARReport.pdf

71   L. Anthony Loman and Gary L. Siegel. (2004). *Minnesota Alternative Response Evaluation: Final Report.* Institute of Applied Research, page 143. Available at: https://www.iarstl.org/papers/ARFinalEvaluationReport.pdf 'Hazard' refers to the relative risk of an undesired outcome, which in this case refers to a child removal.

72   Minnesota: L. Anthony Loman & Gary L. Siegel. (2012). Effects of anti-poverty services under the differential response approach to child welfare. *Children and Youth Services Review, 34,* 1659–1666. For this study, the Cox Proportional Hazards analysis, discussed in reference to Table 3 demonstrated the effect of such services.

73   L. Anthony Loman, Christine Shannon Filonow & Gary L. Siegel. (2010). *Ohio Alternative Response Evaluation: Final Report.* Institute of Applied Research, page 138. Available at: https://www.iarstl.org/papers/OhioAREvaluation.pdf

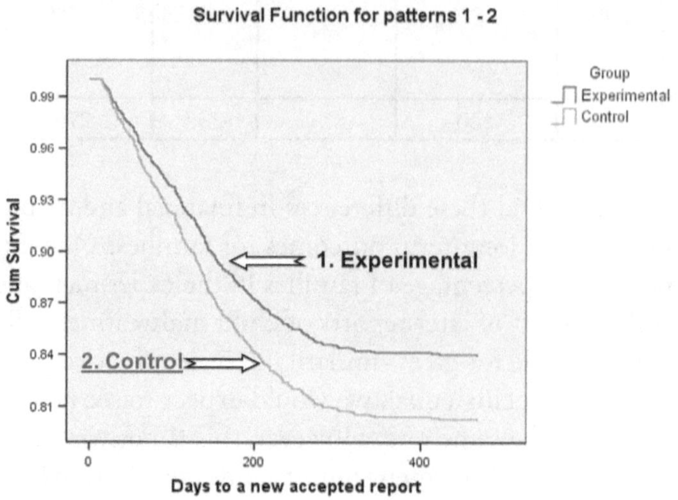

**Figure 4.3. Ohio Proportional Hazards Analysis of
New Accepted Reports of Child Maltreatment**

A nother set of outcomes were indicative. In Ohio, new assessments
of child safety and risk were conducted over a five-year period following
the original intervention. In analyzing subsequent child safety and risk
assessments associated with new child maltreatment reports, we found
the following:

- Children in experimental families were judged to have received
  serious inflicted harm less often.

- Children in experimental families were judged to be less often
  in danger from an adult who was mentally or physically ill.

- Children in experimental families were judged to be less often
  in danger of neglect, including lack of supervision, food,
  clothing or shelter.

- Children in experimental families were less often in families
  that refused access to the child or were likely to flee.

- Children in experimental families were less often found in
  situations of failure to meet their serious physical or mental
  health needs.

Conclusions Regarding the Two DR Studies. These RCT studies used the strongest experimental design, random assignment, creating virtually identical groups of families. Significantly more material support was provided to families in experimental groups. Outcome analysis indicated that the risk and actual occurrence of subsequent child abuse and neglect reports and child removals were substantially reduced over a period of years. The later safety of children, as measured by child safety assessments, was also demonstrated. They provide strong evidence that financial assistance to families experiencing financial hardship can significantly improve the welfare of such families and the safety and welfare of children.

Study 5: The Nevada Differential Response (DR) Evaluation

This study tracked families in a special statewide differential response (DR) program in Nevada.[74] While no extra money was provided for families that entered the program, the structure of the program ensured that they were provided with substantially more material (financially-related) services than standard cases. Families that entered the program had been reported to Child Abuse and Neglect County hotlines. Only those in which there were no children younger than five years could be referred to DR. The types of reports included educational neglect, environmental neglect, physical or medical neglect, improper supervision, or inappropriate discipline with non-severe physical harm. Reports of these kinds, if selected, did not receive a traditional CPS investigation (as described previously) but in this project were instead referred to a Family Resource Center (FRC) office.

The FRCs were in the business of assisting families in neighborhoods that lacked 'the basic necessities of life' and in which various services were unavailable. FRCs operated as Nevada's child welfare agency. The law establishing FRCs stated: "Nevada's most vulnerable families and children live in these neighborhoods [and] many such families not only live in poverty, but also experience divorce or are headed by a single parent.... [Furthermore,] children who are raised in such neighborhoods frequently experience physical and mental abuse."

---

74 Gary L. Siegel, Christine Shannon Filonow & L. Anthony Loman. (2010). *Differential Response in Nevada: Final Report.* Institute of Applied Research. Available at: https://www.iarstl.org/papers/NevadaDRFinalReport.pdf

Services. The Nevada study did not involve a prospectively selected control group. Thus, comparisons of services provided to highly similar groups of experimental and control families, like those in the four previously discussed experiments were not possible. However, we conducted surveys of workers involved with samples of DR families and other workers involved with samples of families that were traditionally investigated. These surveys comparing services typically provided by FRCs in comparison to CPS can be found in the final evaluation report. They show that the FRCs provided substantially more services of all kinds, including material, than CPS. These included emergency food supplies, assistance with transportation, help with household needs (such as utilities, furniture, appliances, etc.), housing, and help with rent or house payments.[75]

Outcomes. At the end of the study, we created a retrospective control group. This occurred because several thousand cases that could have been referred to FRCs were not referred. The selection method matched families that were appropriate for referral to FRC but were not referred on a variety of characteristics recorded in the state child welfare data system. There were 1,861 families referred to FRCs during the study for which full data were available for comparison.[76] This constituted the *experimental group* for subsequent analysis. Only families with a disposition of *investigation* were included in the pool of potential control cases. Initially, two matches were selected for each DR family from among the pool of investigated cases based on paired similarity. These paired cases had child maltreatment reports within 60 days (plus or minus) of the matching experimental family. This group of 3,722 families was submitted to a computer program designed to produce greater *group similarity* between experimental and control families. This was weighted procedure that set families aside in successive steps while comparing experimental and control groups as wholes at each step.

The most important factor in this type of selection process is risk of future child maltreatment. The control group selected was on average equivalent on these measures: previous reports leading to an

---

75   *Ibid.* pages 78-84.
76   A total of 1,903 unduplicated families were referred. Of these, incomplete data were available for 52 families from the Nevada SACWIS system (UNITY) as provided to evaluators.

investigation over about eight years before the initial report in the study (mean per group: E: 1.21, C: 1.26) and previous child removals (mean per group: E: .33, C: .26). Neither of these differences were statistically significant.

No significant differences were found for most areas of allegations associated with previous reports: sexual abuse, severe physical abuse, physical abuse, drug-exposed infant, severe neglect, emotional abuse, medical neglect, unmet medical needs, and lack of supervision. Experimental families were more likely to have been previously reported for neglect of basic needs, such as food, clothing and housing (mean reports, E: mean of .75, C: mean of .57; p = .002) and educational neglect (E: .12, C: .07; p = .005).

Control families on average had slightly more children (E: mean of 2.8 children; C: mean of 3.2 children; p < .001) but slightly more two-parent households (E: mean of 1.74 parents, C: mean of 1.8 parents; p = .003). The former makes comparison families at slightly higher risk for new reports while the latter reduces their risk slightly. In addition, control parents were slightly older. For example, the primary parents/caregivers for experimental families averaged 35.7 years while the same for control families averaged 36.6 years (p < .001). While these differences were statistically significant, the sizes of the differences were small.

There were positive outcomes. Experimental and control families had identical rates of previous investigations (E: 42.5%, C: 42.4%), but experimental families experienced 8.6% fewer subsequent investigations (E: 15.7%, C: 24.3%; p < .001). A survival analysis was conducted in which subsequent investigations of experimental and control families were compared while controlling the level of past investigations (that is, setting the groups equal in terms of risk). This showed a statistically significant difference (p < .001). The same kind of analysis was conducted for any report, whether investigated or not. This analysis also showed improvement for experimental families (p < .001). The analysis showed a reduced relative risk of new reports of any kind for experimental families of .73. This means that for every 100 reports on control families 73 were received on experimental families.

Subsequent removals and placements of children because of new child maltreatment reports after experimental and control case closings occurred at very low rates. There were only 10 children removed from 1,861 experimental families (.05%) compared to 12 children from 1,105 control families (1.1%). The difference in a survival analysis controlling for past removals was statistically significant (p < .001), but because of the small numbers, the results should be regarded with caution.

Conclusions Regarding Nevada. This was the weakest of the studies from an experimental design perspective. Nonetheless, substantial reductions in future reports and investigations of child maltreatment were found for families provided with FRC services.

Study 6: The Minnesota Parent Support Outreach Program (PSOP)

The final study we consider was not a controlled experiment. It was an evaluation study we conducted in Minnesota of the Parent Support Outreach Program (PSOP).[77] The PSOP operated from 2005 to 2008.

In family-oriented field experiments, like the five considered above, control groups are possible when comparable data can be collected on characteristics of families and family members for all potential experimental and control cases. In addition, it must be possible to collect information on members of both groups about program participation and subsequent changes (outcomes) that take place in families. As will be evident in the following, collecting these kinds of data on potential control families was virtually impossible in PSOP study.

On the other hand, the data collected on families that did participate in PSOP was more consistent and detailed than in the previous five. Furthermore, various correlational analyses indicated that providing material resources to families experiencing financial hardship had positive effects on family life and on the safety and welfare of the children.

---

77   L. Anthony Loman, Christine Shannon, Lina Sapakaite & Gary L. Siegel. (2009). *Minnesota Parent Support Outreach Program Evaluation. Institute of Applied Research.* Available at https://www.iarstl. org/papers/PSOPFinalReport.pdf.

The PSOP targeted families who had been reported for child maltreatment. However, in these cases the reports were not accepted by CPS for further action. When child maltreatment telephone hotline reports are received, intake workers question the reporters about what they have observed or heard to determine whether the problems being reported correspond to the state statues governing child abuse and neglect. Examples of reports that do not are: accidents that did not involve parental negligence or malice; family situations that are not dangerous enough to pose safety hazards for children; second-hand knowledge of abuse or neglect incidents; crimes that are real (such as rape) that do not involve neglect or are not perpetrated by relative or family members. There are many others.

The basic idea underlying PSOP was to contact these families to determine whether they needed help and solicit their voluntary participation in services. After the first year of the program the referral process was expanded, permitting families to be referred to the program from other programs, such as the Minnesota Family Investment Program (MFIP), Minnesota's welfare to work program.

The same Minnesota foundation (McKnight) that funded the original Minnesota DR project referenced above, provided extra money for PSOP. Thirty-eight counties participated. In each, a target number of families to be served was set. Each county received $1,000 per target family that could be spent in various ways.

By the conclusion of the study PSOP services had been offered to 7,752 (unduplicated) families of which 3,841 (49.5%) decided to participate. Families with past reports to CPS and/or open CPS cases were *more likely* to accept PSOP services (34.7% of accepters versus 27.7% of decliners). More generally, families that had received services from other agencies such as the Minnesota Child Welfare program, childcare services, services related to developmental disabilities of children and various other adult services tended to accept PSOP services more often.

County program procedures utilizing the funds varied greatly. One of the most interesting findings is that contacted families accepted PSOP services substantially more often (64.3%) in counties that relied on workers from private agencies compared to about half (49.6%) in counties relying on public CPS agency workers. Rates of acceptance among families with previous CPS reports and cases were higher in counties utilizing private agency workers. Nonetheless, the majority of families who participated received services that they would not have received without the outreach program.

There were many indicators of financial hardship. Nearly two-thirds of families (65.3%) were receiving food stamps. More than half had participated in WIC (52.6%). Families who responded to surveys indicated stress about their financial outlook ('A lot': 45.7%, 'Some': 36.7%).

Workers provided assessment data on families. They reported that 59.7% had inadequate incomes or were in poverty. In 13.6%, workers judged that the poverty was extreme and severe. Workers indicated problems associated with employment in 48.6% of families served (underemployment: 13.8%, unemployment: 34.8%). They also noted *chronic* emotional health to be a problem for over a quarter (28.1%) of an adult in families.

Services. The average (mean) number of contacts made with or on behalf of families was 16. Four or more face-to-face contacts were made with 54 percent of families and 11 or more with 18 percent of families. Workers indicated that services were provided directly in many areas related to financial hardship and poverty (for example: basic household needs: 28.3%, emergency food: 15.1%, transportation assistance: 18.8%, medical/dental: 5.3%). In addition, the large majority of families (87.3%) were referred to at least one community service provider (for example: childcare/Head Start: 30.3%, emergency food: 28.9%, mental health: 32.8%, community action agency: 14.2%, legal services: 12.5%, domestic violence shelter: 9.8%, and many others). Families indicated many areas of such service reception (for example: food or clothing 30.2%, money for rent: 19.1%, help paying utilities: 15.3%, childcare: 15.0%, housing: 12.7%, appliance/furniture/home repair: 8.8%, and many others).[78]

Outcomes. Both workers and families generally agreed that the assistance provided fit the needs of families and was effective. Among

---

78   See the above cited final report (note 41). Extensive discussions can be found on pages 45-51, followed by several case examples.

families responding to surveys, 42.5% indicated that they were much better off because of the PSOP experience and another 36.9% said they were somewhat better off. A minority indicated that they were somewhat worse off (17.8%). Concerning needs that they were able to address workers responded that they observed marked improvement in numerous areas. These can be seen in Figure 4.4. Workers indicated that they observed improvements in family income (25.3%) and employment (20.9%), in parent-child relationships (14.8%) and parenting skills (15.3%) and in numerous other areas. Overall, workers noted that marked improvement had occurred in 62.1% of families for at least one of the issues listed in Figure 4.4.

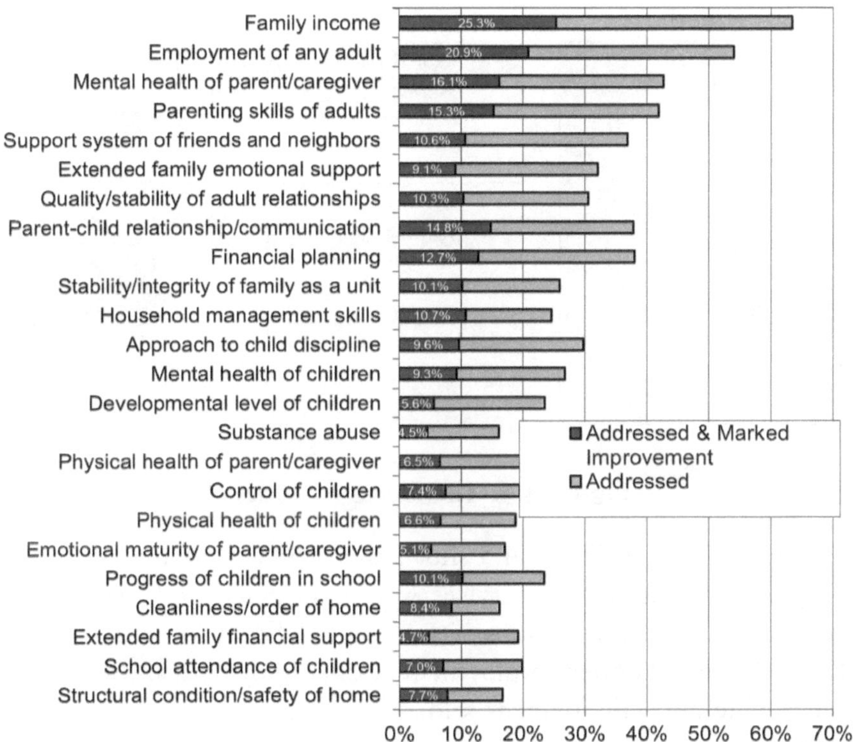

Figure 4.4. Family Functioning Issues Addressed while the PSOP Case was Open and the Proportion in which the Worker Felt there was Marked Improvement

We developed an outcome assessment approach that we called the *dosage model* (see Figure 4.5). The model was based on the assumption that in a program of the magnitude of PSOP, families with similar sets of needs could be found that for different reasons received variable levels of services addressing those needs. If the services were effective, then families that received and utilized more (higher doses) might be expected to have better outcomes than families with less or none. The model was utilized because service and outcome information were collected in sufficient detail along with views of workers and family caregivers concerning the benefits and detriments of the PSOP service approach.

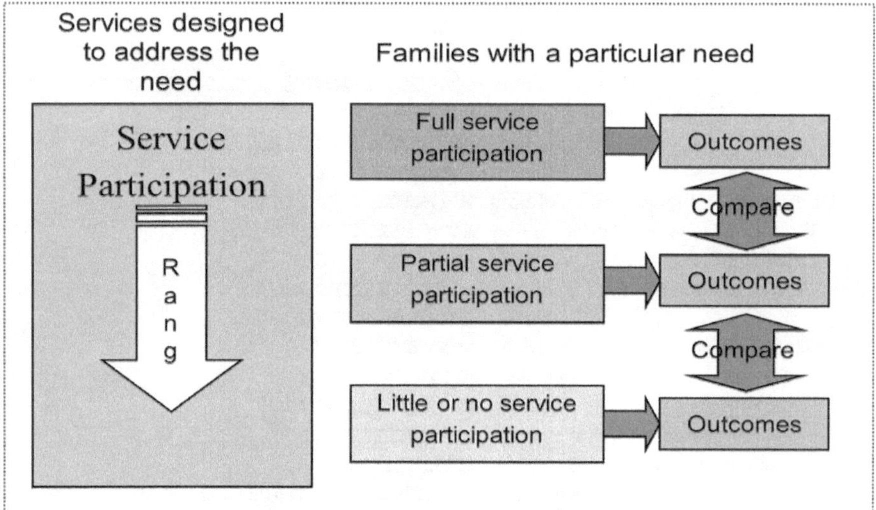

Figure 4.5. The Dosage Model

The diagram in Figure 4.5 shows the approach to analysis in the dosage model. Needs and services were considered and matched in three critical areas,: 1) serious basic needs deficiencies and poverty-related services, 2) under-employment & unemployment and assistance with welfare and employment and training, 3) substance abuse and substance abuse treatment.

Services addressing financial hardship are included in the following list. We considered these to be the strongest contributors to the measure. The needs associated with these services are highly interrelated and arise in part from low income and unemployment.

Rent/house payments	Emergency food	Housing
Basic household needs	Transportation	Employment
Emergency shelter	TANF/SSI/FS	

We also decided to use these because the component services were offered to more PSOP clients than any other kinds of services. Families with high scores on this measure participated in several of these services. Families with lower scores participated in fewer or none of these services. The emphasis was primarily on *participation in* services, which, of course, can only occur after *provision of* services. There were families that were offered many services in this list but that had lower scores on this measure because they used the services at low levels or not at all. This is an important distinction: *only families that utilized services at high levels had high scores on the services measures.* The focus was on something actually delivered to and utilized by a family that might produce a change.

As we have noted, the majority of families accepting PSOP services were in or near poverty and a subset of these were deeply in poverty. There are, however, various mitigating factors. For example, families may have low incomes but some financial support from their extended families or families may receive support from various non-cash programs. The important consideration for this analysis is not poverty per se but need for the kinds of services in the preceding list of services. Thus, we decided to use the measure of needs for basic services that workers completed for each family. There were 1,541 families (86.0 percent) in the *adequate or some problems* category and 250 families (14.0 percent) in the *serious/chronic basic needs deficiency* category.

Families entering PSOP during the first year had two to three years for tracing and follow-up compared to only a few months for most families entering during the third year. As noted, a survival analysis is the stronger approach in studies of this kind in which varying time exists for families to experience a negative outcome—in this case one or more subsequent reports to CPS of child maltreatment. The following chart (Figure 4.6) illustrates this analysis. The lines represent the survival patterns (cumulative survival for each of the four groups over the entire follow-up period (a maximum of approximately

1,150 days). Survival in this case indicates the proportion of families remaining without a new CPS report. *The higher the line the better the outcome.* The difference of interest in this diagram is that between the bottom line representing the group of families with *serious/chronic basic needs with no (or low) basic services* and the other three groups. The difference was statistically significant, as is shown by the variable listing near the bottom of the figure in which the difference between the last variable (the bottom line in the graph) and the other variables is statically significant (p = .05). The analysis indicates that serious or chronic basic needs families did as well as families with fewer needs *when services addressing those needs were utilized* and did significantly worse *when such services were not made available or were not utilized.* The latter had significantly more subsequent CA/N reports screened-in to CPS and the reports were received sooner.

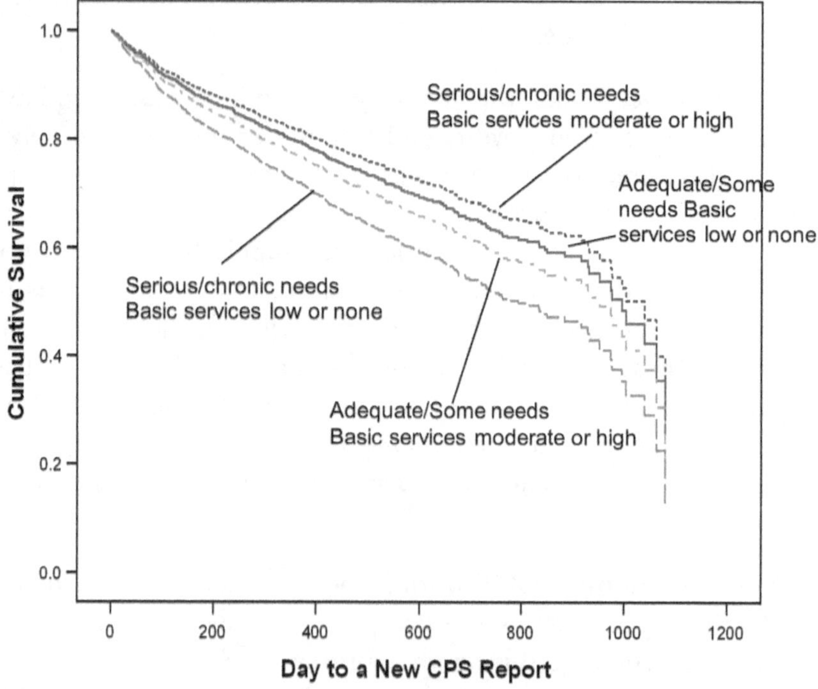

Figure 4.6. Survival Analysis (Proportional Hazards) Low and High Basic Needs by Low and High Poverty-Related Services

This was a correlational analysis, and alternative explanations of the results are possible. Dividing the PSOP families into those with adequate or some basic needs versus those with serious or chronic basic needs certainly has an empirical basis in the judgments of workers that visited and assisted the families. However, within each of these groups the division into service groups of low or none versus moderate or high was based in part on the choice of families to accept and utilize such services and in part on barriers to services beyond their control. It is possible that their willingness and their capacities to overcome barriers reflected other characteristics of families (e.g., attitudes, skills, social support, environmental) that explain to some extent the differences observed.

A similar analysis was conducted based on the much smaller sample of families that responded to the family survey. We divided the families into four groups based on combining those with incomes above and below the $10,000 threshold who received or did not receive poverty related services. We conducted a proportional hazards analysis for these four groups. We controlled for the social isolation of the family and the quality of the neighborhood in which they lived but found no effects on either of these variables on report recurrence. Satisfaction with their PSOP worker was also analyzed and this was associated with a statistical trend (p = .08): families more satisfied when their worker returned less often. Controlling for these three variables a significant relationship was found between poverty-related services and later reductions in subsequent child maltreatment reports (p = .04). The most impoverished families with the least services fared the worst. They were more likely to have new reports and to have them more quickly. Those with higher incomes, who participated in no services fared best. The other two other groups fell in between.

Similar analyses were conducted for employment status and employment related services as well as for substance abuse in the family and substance abuse treatment services. Both these analyses were concluded with similar results.[79]

Summary of the Studies, Conclusions, and Implications

We have examined six studies. Five were experimental. Of these three involved Randomized Control Trials (RCT) and the other two involved matching, one prospective in nature and the other

---

79   These analyses can be found on pages 78-83 in the above cited report (note 41).

retrospective. The sixth was a correlational study included because it involved detailed information from workers about characteristics of families and the types of services delivered to them.

The programs being evaluated in each case involved substantial increases in material services for experimental families and greater flexibility in the application of those services, particularly greater participation of families in the decision-making process. Material services refer to *financially related services,* that is, more money was available in each case to make sure that effects of financial hardship and poverty were addressed. These were the major differences in the experimental studies between experimental and control groups. Thus, any differences observed during years of follow-up on families was almost certainly due to the experimental treatment.

The studies were large, each involving thousands of families. The follow-up periods were long consisting of years for the majority of cases. These two factors add to the strength and validity of study findings. In each study the levels and types of services that constituted the experimental treatment were measured in various ways. Positive outcomes occurred in each study:

- Concerning the safety and welfare of children, each of the studies demonstrated statistically significant reductions in child maltreatment reports that must be attributed to the financial assistance that was offered.

- In several cases, the level of financial assistance was shown to produce stronger effects, that is, reductions in subsequent reports were greater among families receiving higher levels of material services.

- In two studies in which the safety of children was such that imminent removal from their homes was possible significantly reduced out-of-home placement was subsequently observed.

- In addition, length of stays of children in out-of-home placement were reduced among children in placement.

- Statistically significant reductions in subsequent removal and out-of-home placement of children were also observed in four of the studies.

- In one study, evidence of improved family relations and general child welfare was found, including parents reports of improved child development and school performance along with a sense that their children were better off.

- One of the RCT studies considered subsequent safety assessments of children and found:

- Children in experimental families were judged to have received serious inflicted harm less often.

- Children in experimental families were judged to be less often in danger from an adult who was mentally or physically ill.

- Children in experimental families were judged to be less often in danger of neglect, including lack of supervision, food, clothing or shelter.

- Children in experimental families were less often in families that refused access to the child or were likely to flee.

- Children in experimental families were less often found in situations of failure to meet their serious physical or mental health needs.

Implications. The implication of this research is that income maintenance and child protection services should be recombined. This was the approach before the introduction of the Child Abuse Prevention and Treatment Act (CAPTA) in the United States in 1972, when these functions were separated. Workers before those changes were responsible for both functions. When we first began our differential response studies in Missouri in the 1990s, there were still older workers around that remembered the pre-1972 period. They often commented that DR felt like a return to those days when they were concerned with family welfare generally as well as protecting children.

In addition, these studies suggest that financial resources controllable by CPS workers should be expanded to enable financial hardship and poverty to be addressed in families in the less risky end of the current CPS spectrum. Services should definitely continue to address particular child safety issues (for example, reducing the use of corporal punishment, improvement of parenting skills generally, and the like) and removal of children when their lives and health are seriously threatened. However, they should also focus on more basic areas of family needs that are found in large proportions of CPS caseloads, such as housing safety and cleanliness, rent assistance, adequate food and clothing, household items, appliances, transportation assistance, childcare, respite care, and many similar needs and services.

A just rejoinder to this is that CPS and income maintenance are targeted programs. A much broader set of families have similar needs who were never reported to CPS and will never be reported. Yet they also would likely benefit from similar assistance. I agree and we support such general initiatives as a Federal Jobs Guarantee and Universal Basic Income, as discussed below.

Chapter 5

How Financial Hardship is Related to Child Welfare
Generally

In this chapter we will examine studies that demonstrate effects of providing regular and repeated cash to families on the welfare and development of children. In some cases, the programs examined were used with families meeting certain criteria (for example, qualifying for cash welfare). Others concerned large scale public policies regarding taxes and minimum wages that brought more money into families. In still others, money was provided to families without regard to financial need or other characteristics.

Before going on, we should mention the work of Kerris Cooper and Kitty Stewart. Their 2017 paper *Does Money Affect Children's Outcomes? An Update* is a review of 34 studies of outcomes among children, including cognitive, social-behavioral and health, when families experience changes in income.[80] The paper is not long and is worth reading.

A. U.S. Government Family Financial Support: Effects on Children

Various studies were conducted during and after the 1996 Federal reforms of cash welfare programs for families with children. One of these was being completed in Minnesota at the time I and my colleagues were beginning our research in that state that I described in the previous chapter.

In the US, the Aid to Families with Dependent Children program (AFDC) was replaced in 1996 by the Personal Responsibility and

80   Kerris Cooper & Kitty Stewart. (2017). *Does Money Affect Children's Outcomes? An Update.* London: Centre for Analysis of Social Exclusion, London School of Economics. Available at: https://www.jrf.org.uk/report/does-money-affect-children%E2%80%99s-outcomes

Work Opportunity Reconciliation Act (PRWORA). AFDC was a cash welfare program that provided modest cash primarily to mother-only families. It was a way of helping families feed, clothe and house their children, at least minimally. It was effectively a way of providing money to children. PRWORA reduced the cash coming into impoverished families by placing strict time limits on participation. The new payments were dubbed TANF' for Temporary Assistance to Needy Families, with the emphasis on the T. TANF was described in Chapter 1.

Prior to the PRWORA passage several states were permitted to apply for waivers to assess the potential effects of modifying AFDC. If a state's proposed plan was approved, it was permitted to set up a test. Each test program had to be evaluated to determine whether outcomes for families and children changed in any way. The research projects identified the population of families that applied for or were already receiving cash welfare. Families were *randomly assigned* to experimental groups that operated under new conditions or to control groups that basically maintained the existing procedures and rules. The reason these studies are considered here is that some provided additional cash payments to experimental families that were unavailable to control families. Others provided no substantial assistance of this kind but were rather concerned with requiring parents (again, mainly single mothers) to find and maintain employment.

The Minnesota research will give you a taste of what was involved in these studies.[81] The welfare program in Minnesota was named the Minnesota Family Investment Program (MFIP), which began before the 1996 changes in welfare legislation. Under the State's waiver, groups were set up and tracked for three years. Single parent families who were long-term recipients of welfare were selected for the program. In this state, they were randomly assigned to one of three groups.

Group 1 followed the new MFIP rules that 1) permitted more of the earnings of working families to be disregarded in calculating their supplemental benefits. This meant that they had more money than they would have had under AFDC. 2) In addition, childcare expenses were covered and childcare providers were paid directly by the state.

---

81   Lisa A. Gennetian & Cynthia Miller. (2002). Children and Welfare Reform: A View from an Experimental Welfare Program in Minnesota. *Child Development, 73,* 601-620.

3) Also, this group was required to participate in employment and training (E&T) activities designed to help them find a job if they were unemployed or if employed perhaps to find a better job. This requirement was waived for participants who were working 30 hours or more per week. In addition, it was waived for other reasons in a minority of cases, for example, when there was a child in the family under one or the mother was disabled. 4) Finally, the old AFDC money was combined with state support funds and Food Stamps into a single cash payment. Like most welfare programs this one involved complex rules and procedures, but essentially these changes meant more money in the pockets of these families than they would have had under AFDC.

Group 2 followed the rules of the AFDC program and received the traditional benefits and certain benefits of other state financed programs.

Group 3 was set up to distinguish between the two different elements of Group 1: the financial incentives versus the employment requirements. None of the families assigned to this group were required to participate in the employment and training program. Like Group 1, they effectively received more money. This was a particularly thoughtful and useful research design.

One child was randomly selected in each family from among children in the 2- to 9-year age range and was tracked over time. Two-thirds of these kids (66%) were under 6 at the time of random assignment. They were evenly divided by gender (male: 50.8%; female 49.2%) and about half (49.3%) were firstborn children. Three out of ten parents (30.1%) had not finished high school, and the remainder had a high school diploma or GED (57.7%) or some higher education (12.1%). As noted, they were generally long-term AFDC recipients: 75.2% had been in the program for two years or more. They were families in poverty.

Here is what the study found after operating for three years. The earnings of families in groups 1 and 3 increased compared to group 2. Participation in MFIP led to increased use of formal child-care centers. Utilization of centers was 18% higher for these families compared to the control group. Regarding family relationships, physical and non-physical domestic abuse declined in the MFIP participating families by 11%. No differences were found for measures of parental depression. However, MFIP increased parental supervision of children and knowledge of the children's whereabouts while they were away from home. Compared to the control group, children in the MFIP groups had significantly fewer social behavioral problems, things like being disobedient or cruel, throwing temper tantrums or breaking things. The children scored significantly higher on school engagement. They also performed better in school (a statistical trend only). By comparing Groups 1 and 3, the researchers were able to show that the positive results were *not due to employment requirements. Increased money was the cause of the positive changes.*

These kinds of studies were also conducted in other states. A paper by Clark-Kauffman and associates considered similar research in seven states and included the Minnesota study.[82] Some of the projects involved earnings supplements, like Minnesota, that increased the cash available to families. Others simply tacked on participation in employment and training activities to the old AFDC requirements.

It is not necessary to describe these programs here. However, one finding is relevant. In the programs providing cash increases, families received additional money in the range of $1,500 to $2,000 per year. Others that emphasized E&T provided no or only minimal cash supplements, never more than $250 per year. The researchers separated the effects of these two approaches in their analysis. When assessments were conducted of families 2 to 5 years after they entered the programs, it was found that offering generous cash supplements to experimental families led to improvements in children's cognitive performance and/ or school achievement. The differences were seen primarily among preschool children (ages 0-2 and 3-5 years at the time of entry into the study).

Another later paper by Duncan and associates reviewed and reanalyzed many of the same experiments but also examined other studies including two similar projects in Canada. Again, they found improved cognitive performance as reported by parents and teachers

82   Elizabeth Clark-Kauffman, Greg J. Duncan & Pamela Morris. (2003). How welfare policies affect children and adolescent achievement. *American Economic Review,* 93, 299–303.

and in some cases by test scores but only among families that received earnings supplements. The correlation between increasing annual income and child achievement scores is presented graphically and convincingly in the article.[83]

There was some puzzlement in these two summary papers as to how to explain the cognitive gains among children. For example, in the Minnesota study, how did the reductions in domestic violence and increases in supervision of children produce better school performance? We can easily imagine ways this might have occurred in some families, but why such a strong finding?

In the Duncan review the authors speculated about possible causes of the positive cognitive changes in children. One thought was that the increased utilization of childcare centers might have been important. As an example, the increase cited for the Minnesota study was substantial. The researchers in Minnesota also found that childcare center usage was more consistent and occurred for longer periods of time when it was provided by the State. I learned about the preferences of poor mothers in a study of childcare we conducted in Illinois. We were studying the effects of making childcare available to mothers on welfare.[84] A pervasive idea at that time was that impoverished mothers did not want to put their children in formal childcare arrangements if they could avoid it. Instead, it was thought that they preferred childcare by relatives. We found, on the contrary, that impoverished mothers, like most mothers, preferred formal childcare centers, although few could afford them.[85] This preference was reaffirmed again in the Minnesota study just described. The older notion arose by confusing necessity with preference. Poor mothers can seldom afford formal center fees and formal centers are often not available in or near their neighborhoods. The increase in use of centers in the welfare reform experiments may have been an important factor in explaining improved academic performance of children, particularly in children younger than six. Centers have employees that supervise and interact with the children

<hr>

83 Greg J. Duncan, Pamela Morris & Chris Rodrigues. (2011). Does money really matter? Estimating impacts of family income on young children's achievement with data from random- assignment experiments. *Developmental Psychology, 47,* 1263–79.

84 Gary L. Siegel & L. Anthony Loman. (1991). *Child Care and AFDC Recipients in Illinois.* Institute of Applied Research. The digest of the study is available at: http://www.iarstl.org/papers/IllinoisChildCare.pdf

85 *Ibid.* Look on pages 13 and 14 for this material.

as part of their job. Many also have books and educational toys and equipment. Very importantly, centers are places where children from impoverished families can meet other children from families with more resources. The influence of peers on children begins early and increases as they age. Of course, this is speculation and does not prove *what* caused the improvements, although one of the studies on the effects of formal preschool in Chapter 1 appears to support this interpretation.[86] Nonetheless, not conclusively proving *how* does not detract from the fact that increased money in impoverished families leads to positive improvements in children's cognitive and academic performances.

The studies just considered in which benefits to families and children *increased* were experimental in nature. They *do not* represent what happened subsequently as PRWORA was implemented and TANF replaced AFDC across the US. In 1996, as TANF was implemented, 68% of families in poverty across the United States received such assistance. By 2017 the percentage had declined to just 23%, and the percentage was only that high because of more generous support in states such as California, New York and the state we looked at above in more detail, Minnesota.[87] In these states, the percentages were greater than 40%. The experimental studies just considered consistently confirmed that more cash improves child welfare and development. TANF created barriers to program participation and thus effectively reduced cash to millions of impoverished families and children. Putting money into families improves child welfare. Taking money out reverses the process and damages the welfare of children.

Two studies in other countries are worth considering in this context. First, a welfare program, called *Oportunidades*, was introduced in Mexico and has been the subject of multiple studies. One of these by Manley and associates looked at the physical and cognitive changes in children based on transfers of money.[88] Under *Oportunidades*, poor households received payments that were conditioned on household

---

86   Elizabeth U. Cascio. (2019). *Does Universal Preschool Hit the Target? Program Access and Preschool Impacts*. Dartmouth College. Available at: https://www.nber.org/papers/w23215

87   IFE Floyd, Ashley Burnside & Liz Schott. (2018). *TANF Reaching Few Poor Families*. Center for Budget and Policy Priorities. Available at: https://www.cbpp.org/research/family-income-support/tanf-reaching-few-poor-families

88   James G. Manley, Lia C. H. Fernald & Paul J. Gertler. (2015). Wealthy, healthy and wise: Does money compensate for being born into difficult conditions? *Applied Economics Letters, 22(2)*, 121-126. Available at: http://dx.doi.org/10.1080/13504851.2014.929618

members accepting medical check-ups, sending the children to school and attending education discussions with care providers. The study employed a quasi-experimental design, and the analysis was thoughtfully and carefully conducted. Statistically significant changes were observed between the experimental and control groups in the children's height for age, Body Mass Index (BMI) and verbal scores on the Wechsler Abbreviated Scale of Intelligence (WASI). A statistical trend was found in improved cognitive WASI scores. The researchers demonstrated that effects on children were due to the additional cash received rather than length of time in the program.

Another study by Raschke that analyzed the effects of the German Child Benefit program is relevant.[89] In Germany families are taxed only on income that exceeds the *living wage* level. In that system living wage is calculated based on the cost of food, housing, transportation and a portion for unexpected expenses. The amount calculated represents a non-taxable base income. The child benefit is in addition to this and is conceptually something like the US tax deduction for dependents but with a major difference. It is not calculated when paying taxes. Instead, each family receives a monthly cash payment based on the number of children in the home. The payment is not dependent on family income levels or any other family characteristics but is available to every family with children. In this sense, the program is closer to a Universal Basic Income (UBI) program, as considered below. Importantly, the child benefit runs up through age 25, sufficient to assist families whose children have graduated high school and are attending higher education.

The Raschke study was also quasi-experimental, analyzing eleven years of economic data (1998 to 2009) and the results of regular surveys of participating families. The author makes a case for *labeling* of cash sources, which is a kind of mental notation that parents make, and argues that differences observed arose from the particular cash source being investigated. The benefit was responsible for the following effects. Increased benefits produced increased expenditure on food. They were also related to housing. Increasing benefits led to larger apartments and

---

89   Christian Raschke. (2012) *The Impact of the German Child Benefit on Child Well-Being.* Louisiana State University, Baton Rouge, Department of Economics. SOEPpaper No. 520. Available at: https://ssrn.com/abstract=2197764

more rooms in living quarters. They also were related to a decreased likelihood of renting and thus an increase in home ownership. Given what I noted in Chapter 1 regarding the effects of quality of living arrangements and overcrowding on child welfare and development, these are important findings. We return to the German program and describe the benefits further when we look at solutions.

B. Effects of Poor Wages on Infant Mortality

What about the health of children? The *Oportunidades* program showed positive effects on children's height for age and their body mass index (BMI). An important study by Komro and associates examined possible effects of minimum wage differences among US states on post-neonatal infant mortality and birth weight.[90] As the researchers point out excess infant deaths between the first month and the first year (28 to 364 days) after birth occurs largely among low socioeconomic status (SES) mothers. Infant mortality is strongly associated with low birth weight. In other words, when examining cases of deaths of babies, we find large numbers who had low birth weights, and this is also associated with poverty.

The Komro study examined whether *increases* in the legal minimum wage of various states might *reduce low birth-weight births and infant mortality*.[91] Looking at all 50 US states, 206 legal changes in state minimum wage were found during the 1980 to 2011 period. These were changes states made that were independent of any changes in the federal minimum wage. The difference compared to the federal standard was not great, averaging only approximately $1.00/hour more than the federal minimum wage during the months in which the laws were in effect. Of course, this would amount to $40 a week or approximately $2,000 a year for full-time employment. That would be a maximum value since many minimum wage jobs are not full-time. Health improvements were observed when this occurred. They found that in states that had legislated minimum wage increases:

---

90   Kelli A. Komro, Melvin D. Livingston, Sara Markowitz & Alexander C. Wagenaar. (2016). The Effect of An Increased Minimum Wage on Infant Mortality and Birth Weight. *American Journal of Public Health, 106*(8), 1514-1516.

91   *Ibid.* The method is difference in difference multiple regression. In this case, outcomes before and after increases in legal minimum wages in states enacting such laws were compared to changes in states that did not increase their minimum wage. Differences among states comparing before-after differences were analyzed, thus difference in difference,

- Low birth weight births declined significantly as did post-neonatal infant mortality.

Based on their findings, they estimated that if all states had increased their minimum wages by one dollar per hour there would have been 2,790 fewer low birth weight births in 2014 and 518 fewer post-neonatal deaths that year alone. Something that immediately jumps to mind is what would have been the effects of a $2.00 or $10.00 increase?

C. Earned Income Tax Credit (EITC)

The Earned Income Tax Credit (EITC) is a large program that began in 1975 and was expanded in the 1980's and early 1990's. It provided a federal tax refund to families with low incomes, and with the demise of cash welfare assistance as previously described. It is now the largest source of cash assistance in the United States. Several quasi-experimental studies have been conducted to determine whether the credit leads to improvements in the welfare of children in families receiving it. Since the more children in families the greater the tax credit received, it is possible to compare the outcomes for families with varying EITC payments that are otherwise highly similar.

A study by Hilary Hoynes and associates examined the effects of EITC on children's health, specifically low-birthweight births.[92] They found that the increases in EITC (in 1993) led to:

- Declines of 2-3% in low birthweight births.

William Evans and Craig Garthwaite showed positive health-related improvements among low-educated mothers with two children (higher EITC) compared to similar mothers with only one child (lower EITC).[93] Specifically:

---

92   Hilary Hoynes, Doug Miller & David Simon. (2015). Income, the Earned Income Tax Credit, and Infant Health. *American Economic Journal: Economic Policy, 7, 1,* 172-211. An earlier study also examined the effects of the EITC on infant birth weight, showing that increased EITCs increased birth weight and reduced maternal smoking. Kate W. Strully, David H. Rehkopf & Xuan Ziming. (2010). Effects of Prenatal Poverty on Infant Health: State Earned Income Tax Credits and Birth Weight. *American Sociological Review, 74, 4,* 534-562.

93   William Evans & Craig Garthwaite. (2010). *Giving Mom a Break: The Impact of Higher EITC Payments on Maternal Health.* National Bureau of Economic Research. Available at: https://www.nber.org/papers/w16296

- Reported days of poor mental health declined and

- The number of days with excellent or very good health improved.

D. Universal Basic Income

Increases in money to families with children in the welfare reform studies were dependent on income levels and employment. Minimum wage increases apply mainly to individuals who are living near or below poverty levels. What would happen if we simply disregarded such distinctions, many of which are invidious and potentially prejudicial, and distributed money equally to all? This is not a new idea and there are many names for it including: Basic Income (BI), Basic Income Guarantee (BIG), Universal Basic Income (UBI), Citizen's Income, Citizens Basic Income, and others. The third name from this list is used here. UBI is based on the idea that individual citizens (usually adults) will be paid a certain amount of money on a regular basis. The payments are equivalent for each person and are not conditioned on characteristics of the person being paid. Full-time employed, part-time employed, and unemployed people are paid the same. The payment is not affected by marital status or current income levels (like food stamps) or disabilities (like SSI). Both men and women receive payments. Readers who are unaware of this movement will be amazed at the prodigious volume of literature describing and debating this idea and the number of people writing about it. The best international website is BIEN (Basic Income Earth Network: https://basicincome.org/). In the United States there is US BIG (U.S. Basic Income Guarantee: https://usbig.net/).

Experimental programs have been conducted in various states, regions and countries that have provided financial payments to families without regard to their current income or wealth. Much has been written about these, with proposals to expand them permanently. Here are five books about UBI that are worth perusing: Rutger Bregman's, *Utopia for Realists: How We Can Build the Ideal World; Andrew Yang's The War on Normal People; Annie Lowrey's Give People Money: How a Universal Basic Income Would End Poverty, Revolutionize Work, and Remake the World; and, Guy Standing's Basic Income: A Guide for the Open-Minded.* Guy Standing has promoted the idea for decades and was one of the founders of BIEN, when the 'E' stood for European. A more recent book is The Case for Universal Basic Income by the co-chair of BIEN, Louise Haagh.[94] These are all well-known books. I list several more recent ones in Chapter 8 under Solution 3, UBI.

D1. Cherokee Children

This is a study of the effects of basic income among Cherokee children that compares children in Eastern Cherokee Indian families living on the reservation in North Carolina with children in non-Indian families in the same region. Anyone who has read any of the first four books just mentioned will already be familiar with the study because it is described in each. It was a longitudinal study of child mental health that followed children in North Carolina for several years. The study included samples of Cherokee and non-Indian children selected in 1993. Longitudinal studies that track and observe samples (cohorts) over time are referred to as panel studies. The ages of the children were 9, 11 and 13 years at the time of assignment and these constituted age cohorts for the study.[95]

During the study something happened for Cherokee Indian families that permitted a comparative analysis of Basic Income. It was the kind of serendipitous happening that most researchers would love, because it permitted a comparative study of the effects of money on children. In 1997, the reservation established a casino, and the decision was made to distribute some of the profits to all Indian adult tribal members as regular payments. Each Indian adult ended up receiving an average of $4,000 per year. Thus, families with two Indian parents received a yearly average of $8,000. (I did not receive any money, even though my great, great grandmother was an Eastern Cherokee.☺)

For our purposes here, it is important to note that, on average, the Indian households spent at least one year in poverty during the

---

94   Rutger Bregman. (2017). *Utopia for Realists: How We Can Build the Ideal World.* New York: Little, Brown; Andrew Yang. (2018). *The War on Normal People.* New York: Hachette Books; Annie Lowrey. (2018). *Give People Money: How a Universal Basic Income Would End Poverty, Revolutionize Work, and Remake the World.* New York: Random House; Guy Standing. (2017). *Basic Income: A Guide for the Open-Minded.* New Haven: Yale Univ Press; Louise Haagh. (2019). *The Case for Universal Basic Income.* Medford, MA: Polity Press.

95   Randall K. Q. Akee, William E. Copeland, Gordon Keeler, Adrian Angold & E. Jane Costello. (2010). Parents' Incomes and Children's Outcomes: A Quasi-experiment Using Transfer Payments from Casino Profits. *American Economic Journal: Applied Economics, 2,* 86–115.

first three years of the study. During this period the mean Cherokee household earned ($20,919) nearly $10,000 less that the non-Indian ($30,377).

The study collected information on families and children regularly. The experimental group consisted of American Indian children in families receiving increased money. The researchers showed that the three age panels were similar in many ways in each of the two populations being studied. However, they utilized statistical techniques to equalize the characteristics of children and families in Indian and non-Indian households. The issue of historical or time-changes (for example, the effects of changing economic conditions) that we referred to in Chapter One, was controlled using the non-Indian group and the analysis indicated that the two types of households were equally affected by ongoing socioeconomic conditions. Similarly, the groups were and remained alike in household composition.[96] Readers who examine the detailed analyses will be reasonably assured that rough equivalence was achieved and that the subsequent comparisons of children and families were acceptable and demonstrated real effects of increased money in families.

Here is what they found. Some education variables were not statistically significant, but the analysis showed that the increased income among Indian families due to the infusion of casino money increased a child's probability of finishing high school by nearly 15%.

When children in households that had experienced poverty at some time during the three years prior to the casino opening were tracked, the educational effects were highly statistically significant for years of education completed and for graduating from high school. No difference between male and female children appeared for years of education—both showed positive effects. However, the girls had a higher probability of finishing high school than boys. The effects of this analysis occurred when mothers were the recipients of the cash but not when fathers were the recipients. Possibly mothers were more likely to invest more in their children, but data for this possible cause were not available. School attendance was also shown to have increased and

---

96   *Ibid.* The study also used a difference-in-difference regression technique as described in the previous
     notes on the Komro (2016) study.

again this was especially true in the case of families that had previously experienced poverty.

Regarding criminal behavior, children in households receiving casino cash had an 18% lower probability of having committed a minor crime than children in homes not receiving cash. The money did not appear to have affected the *number* of crimes but simply whether *any* crimes were committed. Based on self-reports about their behavior, children in casino cash households were 7% less likely to have been involved in drug dealing.

The researchers were interested, of course, in changes in activities in families that might explain these effects. For instance, did the extra money permit parents to get their children into better educational programs? This question could not be answered because no data were collected about educational programs. Another idea is that the infusion of cash might have permitted mothers to work fewer hours and spend more time helping their children? Interestingly, for those who think that giving money to families might lead to idleness, labor force participation rates of mothers *did not change*. Perhaps the parenting behavior simply improved when more money became available. There was evidence in the study that this happened for parents, both individually and jointly. Supervision of children and reported positive interactions with them improved for both mothers and fathers. Another finding concerning ongoing behavior and choices of parents was that increased money led to a lower probability of the mother or the father being arrested by law enforcement. The study provided strong evidence that regular infusion of money has positive consequences for children, particularly children in impoverished families.

D2. The Canadian Mincome Project

This experiment in Universal Basic Income (UBI) took place in Canada in the 1970's and looked for effects of a guaranteed annual income (GAI), another name for UBI. Like the Cherokee study just described, it was aimed at the entire population, in this case, all the families in the town of Dauphin in Manitoba province. The experiment is described in several of the books on UBI mentioned in the introduction to this section. I include it here because quasi-experimental analyses were subsequently conducted of the voluminous data collected on Dauphin families.

Evelyn Forget of the University of Manitoba was responsible for retrieving the data from the study, some 30 years after it ended. Mincome operated from 1974 to 1979 until a conservative government came into power in Canada, canceled the project and denied money, even for analysis of the voluminous data collected on outcomes for Dauphin residents. Dr. Forget finally found the data in 2009, after five years of searching, in paper files stored in 1,800 boxes in a government archive. At the time, officials were considering destroying the material because no one seemed interested in it! So much of our knowledge seems to be based on happenstance and luck, but Forget's efforts show the value of persistence.

In her 2011 paper analyzing the data, *The Town with No Poverty: The Health Effects of a Canadian Guaranteed Annual Income Field Experiment*, Forget recounts both the history and her analysis.[97] She notes that proponents of a Guaranteed Annual Income saw it as a way to eliminate the so-called *welfare trap,* the assumption that having an income test to qualify for welfare creates a strong disincentive to leave welfare rolls for work. Forget points out that the proponents of the field experiment accurately saw that there were "overlaps and gaps between programs that allowed some families to qualify under two or more programs while others fell between programs." Proponents also correctly noted that the poverty of the working poor was very difficult to overcome. Finally, they also believed that it would be more cost-efficient to offer payments through one bureaucracy as opposed to several.

What Forget does not note is that a single payment to everyone would eliminate the humiliation of applicants (through constant checkups to insure there is no cheating on earned income, forced participation in job-search programs, requiring proofs of disabilities, forced drug tests, etc.) that are common elements of US welfare programs of all kinds. Someone has noted that on one side of the political spectrum there is the assumption that poor and near-poor

---

97   Evelyn Forget. (2011). The Town with No Poverty: The Health Effects of a Canadian Guaranteed Annual Income Field Experiment. *Canadian Public Policy – Analyse de Politiques, 37, 3,* 283-305. Available at: https://www.utpjournals.press/doi/pdf/10.3138/cpp.37.3.283

individuals are lazy. The statistics presented earlier give the lie to this assumption. The poor and near poor do work. On the other side, there is the assumption that poor and near poor are stupid, too dumb to know what is good for them. Therefore, they must be guided and directed—through budgeting classes, decisions by service workers without input from recipients, instruction in how to dress and talk to their class superiors especially when seeking work, and so on. The effectiveness of abandoning these demeaning assumptions were described under the Differential Response approach described in above demonstrating the success of permitting parents to provide their own input into decisions that were made and the particular kinds of assistance needed in child welfare cases.[98]

The Manitoba project was generally designed along the lines of the US experiments described in the next section, although in the US families for the experimental group were randomly sampled and then matched with similar control families. The Dauphin project was a *saturation* site in that every family in the town and surrounding rural areas numbering about 12,500 was to receive a GAI check. Families with no other income would receive 60% of the Canadian low-income cutoff, with reductions of 50 cents for each dollar received from other sources. Families qualifying for public assistance would receive about the same level of support. The elderly, the working poor and single males would see a significant increase in income. GAI reception continued from 1974 through 1978.

The only part of the study that had been analyzed in the fifteen years following the project's demise concerned labor force participation. There was interest in whether supplying people with cash would lead them to drop out of the labor force. Would people who are currently working continue to work when substantial money was simply given to them? The findings were like those of the Cherokee study—very little change in labor force participation. Men worked about 1% fewer hours and women worked 3% fewer hours. An exception to this concerned married women who stayed out of the workforce longer

---

98   A full analysis of this can be read in the final follow-up report of the Ohio evaluation. L. Anthony Loman & Gary L. Siegel. (2014). *Ohio Alternative Response Evaluation Extension: Final Report*. Institute of Applied Research. Available at: http://www.iarstl.org/papers/OhioARFinalExtensionReportFINAL. pdf The relevant material is in Chapter 2, pages 10ff.

when they gave birth.[99] We should note that study after study around the world has found the same thing: ***a guaranteed income does not lead to idleness.*** You can read about this in any of the books on UBI cited here and in Chapter 8.

Later researchers, including Forget, utilized health data from the province in their analysis. Since no community comparable to Dauphin existed in Manitoba, they selected carefully matched control cases from a variety of communities around the province.[100] Here is what the analysis showed. The rate of hospitalization of Dauphin residents declined by 8.5% compared to controls mostly because of reduced accidents, injuries and mental health services, all problems shown in past research to be negatively correlated with socioeconomic status (SES). Hospitalizations are generally indicators of poor health, but contacts with physicians were also reduced. The latter is a somewhat poorer health measure, presumably because some doctor visits simply represent regular health checkups. These reductions represented an improvement from previously poorer comparative measures of health in Dauphin in 1970.

More children continued into grade 12. This change was particularly telling because the differences showed up precisely matched with the 1974-78 period of increased income. This finding corresponds to positive outcomes in the Cherokee study and the welfare reform experiments.

No evidence was found of improvements in fertility, that is, more money did not lead to more children being born. Unlike what we saw in the studies of minimum wage and EITC, no difference was found in birth outcomes as measured by low income or infant deaths. However, it must be noted that Canada, unlike the US, had universal health insurance during this period. Thus, prenatal care was provided to all pregnant women in Manitoba. There was no increase in family dissolutions.

A subsequent paper on Mincome by David Calnitsky, *"More Normal than Welfare": The Mincome Experiment, Stigma, and*

---

99   Derek Hum & Wayne Simpson. (1993). Whatever happened to Canada's guaranteed income project? *Canadian Public Administration / Administration publique du Canada 36,3,* 442-450.

100   They matched on hard characteristics, like age and sex, and also used propensity score matching, as referenced in Chapter 2.

Community Experience examined community attitudes about the project.[101] The study is freely available and is particularly relevant to my earlier comments regarding the *deserving* versus the *undeserving* poor. Calnitsky went into the archived data and analyzed qualitative surveys of Dauphin participants. His paper lists numerous comments showing the motivation of Mincome participants. He categorized them in several different ways: 1. a need for money (e.g., "I needed more money to support the boys."), 2. Security if unable to find work or in case of illness (e.g., "To back up my financial state in case of sickness." or "Because if I ever get laid off I could live."); 3. Could not find work (e.g., "No work at the time, no income."); 4. Could not work because disabled, ill or elderly (e.g., "(John) had broken his leg and we needed help." or "We had no other choice as my husband is disabled and with my health and age, I am unable to work full time…"); 5. To help care for family (e.g., "My children were young and I felt I was needed at home" or "I wasn't eligible for welfare and had to support my son somehow."); 6. Help in going to school (e.g., "We have a chance to improve our educational level in order to improve our income.") 7. Better than welfare (e.g., "Because it offered more independence with money than welfare."). What the study found is that Mincome did not lead to the social stigma associated with welfare programs. Offering financial assistance to everyone regardless of their current income, wealth or employment does away with the moral consideration of who does and does not *deserve help*. In this sense it resembles Social Security in the United States, which is essentially a welfare program for the elderly paid for by younger workers. Franklin Roosevelt removed moral considerations associated with social security by making it universal and by casting it as contributory. When Universal Basic Income is instituted, moralistic prohibitions fade away.

D3. Experiments in the United States

Those who are unfamiliar with Basic Income studies and the many books written about it are also usually unaware that several UBI experiments were conducted in the US during the late 1960's and 1970's. Unlike the studies just described, the US programs that were studied were restricted to low-income populations. They were

---

101 David Calnitsky. (2016). "More Normal than Welfare": The Mincome Experiment, Stigma, and Community Experience. *Canadian Review of Sociology*, 53,1, 26-71. Available at: https://onlinelibrary.wiley.com/doi/pdf/10.1111/cars.12091

studies of negative income tax, like the EITC benefit described earlier. However, they were large scale *prospective field experiments,* like the welfare reform studies and like our experiments described in the previous chapter. For those who are interested in details, a full review of the studies was produced by Robert Levine and Associates as a chapter in a later book.[102] I draw on that paper in the following. A brief history of the US efforts can also be found in Forget's 2011 paper cited above. A fascinating account of how an analysis (that turned out to be erroneous) of an early 19th century anti-poverty effort was used by Richard Nixon to reject income guarantee can be found in the fourth chapter of Rutger Bregman's book cited earlier and also in more historical detail in a chapter by Fred Block and Margaret Somers in the same book in which the Levine and associates paper is found.[103]

As part of his War on Poverty, Lyndon Johnson instituted the Office of Economic Opportunity (OEO). Under it several experiments designed to measure the effects of a negative income tax were initiated in American cities and rural areas. The OEO was later abolished by Richard Nixon, although Nixon himself promoted the idea of a guaranteed income during the early years of his tenure as President. The big concern was that supplying poor folks with money would lead to lower labor supply by reducing labor force participation, which is a technical way of reiterating the idea that poor people, who are assumed to be lazy, will use free money as a pretext to avoid working. There was concern expressed later by politicians ideologically opposed to UBI that families receiving such cash were cheating (double dipping) by hiding their simultaneous participation in cash welfare programs.

Starting in 1968, four experiments were conducted: the New Jersey/Pennsylvania study of urban populations, the Gary Indiana study of single parents, the North Carolina/Iowa study of rural populations, and the Seattle/Denver income maintenance study. The research found that there was a reduction in work effort among families. It amounted to 13 percent but two-thirds of this came from secondary and tertiary

---

102 Robert A. Levine, Harold Watts, Robinson Hollister, Walter Williams, Alice O'Connor & Karl Widerquist. (2016). A Retrospective on the Negative Income Tax Experiments: Looking Back at the Most Innovative Field Studies in Social Policy." Chapter 5 in *The Ethics and Economics of the Basic Income Guarantee,* ed. Karl Widerquist, Michael Anthony Lewis & Steven Pressman. New York: Routledge. The book was originally published in 2005 by Ashgate Publishing.

103 Fred Block & Margaret Somers. (2016). In the Shadow of Speenhamland: Social Policy and the Old Poor Law. Chapter 2 in *The Ethics and Economics of the Basic Income Guarantee,* ed. Karl Widerquist, Michael Anthony Lewis & Steven Pressman. New York: Routledge.

earners, working women delaying return to work after an absence and other family members, such as youths, working less. So, the actual difference for primary earners was small.

Subsequent analysis of the Seattle-Denver study demonstrated that an earlier analysis showing very high marriage-dissolution rates of 57% among experimental families receiving cash was in error. No such difference occurred and no differences in subsequent studies, like the Dauphin experiment just described, have been found in divorces and separations in experimental versus control families.

Here are some findings relevant to the welfare and development of children. In North Carolina, attendance rates in grades 2 through 8 increased, teacher ratings of students rose, and test score improved. In the Levine chapter cited earlier, Robert Hollister notes that the educational literature shows the difficulty in raising test scores by working directly with learners. This reminded me of a topic mentioned previously regarding social work with families alleged to have maltreated their children. Duncan Lindsey in his book on child welfare conducted an analysis that illustrated the ineffectiveness of social work with such families under the traditional system utilizing the residual approach. Yet I and my colleagues demonstrated in large *experimental* studies that supplying cash to families produced positive outcomes.

The New Jersey study showed a significant effect on school continuation, that is, reduced dropouts from schools, another outcome in which cash to families had an effect in contrast to direct efforts to work with youths to stay in school, which have generally been ineffective. Remember that this was also found in the North Carolina Cherokee study.

The Gary study showed that the incidence of low birthweight rates declined in the most at-risk categories. This was an early confirmation of the findings of later studies on minimum wage and EITC. In the first year of the Gary experiment and in New Jersey and in the North Carolina/Iowa rural studies home ownership was achieved more often by experimental families. This corresponds to the German study on the effects of their Child Benefit program.

Chapter 6

Summary of Outcome Findings of Field Experiments

In this short chapter I summarize what was found in the experimental studies that were reviewed previously.

In Chapter 4, two RCT experimental studies in Minnesota and Ohio of the differential response approach to child protection were reviewed. Experimental families received more material resources than control families. In both states subsequent reports of child maltreatment dropped for experimental families. Relative improvements were found among experimental families in parenting and in areas normally considered as child neglect (supervision, basic needs, unsafe homes and medical treatment). These differences held up for several years after the original cases had closed.

Two other experiments conducted in Indiana and Mississippi focused on children removed from their homes or in danger of removal. In both states more money and material support were received by experimental families in comparison to control families. In Indiana fewer experimental children in danger of removal were subsequently removed and more experimental children who had been removed from their homes were reunited with their families. Fewer subsequent child abuse and neglect reports were received for experimental families. Reported school performance improved among experimental children. In Mississippi subsequent accepted child abuse and neglect reports decreased significantly and substantially on the experimental side. The greatest differences were found for children who actually received services. Experimental children who remained with their parents were subsequently removed less often.

The material and financial support in these four projects was often modest, involving temporary and one-time assistance. Yet, significant and sometimes substantial positive effects for children were observed. The resources that money can buy did seem to help children.

Chapter 5 was concerned with experimental studies of programs that provided extra money on a more regular basis. A study of welfare reform in Minnesota considered the effects of increases in total cash benefits, including additional help with childcare. Participation in formal childcare centers increased substantially. Experimental children showed significantly fewer behavioral problems, such as disobedience, cruelty, throwing temper tantrums, breaking things. Children scored higher in school engagement and performed better in school. Two other summary analyses considered similar experiments in other states that tested new approaches to welfare. One of the consistent effects found in these studies was that providing cash supplements led to improvements in children's cognitive performance and/or school achievement. In a study in Mexico, poor households received payments that were conditioned on household members accepting medical check-ups, sending the children to school and attending education discussions with care providers. The study found Improvements in the children's height for age, improvements in children's BMI, and increases in their verbal intelligence and cognitive scores. A study of the German Child Benefit program found increased expenditures for food, larger apartments and more rooms in living quarters, and thus less crowding, a decreased likelihood of renting and an increase in home ownership.

A study of state increases in minimum wage above the federal level found that low birth weight births declined significantly and post-neonatal infant mortality declined.

Studies of the Earned Income Tax Credit (EITC) found that the Behavior Problem Index (BPI) of children improved due to larger EITC payments, and the quality of a children's home environment increased. Another study found that increased money through EITC lowered low-birthweight births significantly, by an estimated 2-3%. Another study found that reported days of poor mental health declined and the number of days with excellent or very good health increased for low-educated mothers receiving additional cash through EITC. Certain health biomarkers also improved.

A study of a form of Universal Basic Income (UBI) among Eastern Cherokee Indian families in North Carolina found that regular cash payments increased the probability of a child finishing high school by about 15%. School attendance was shown to have increased, especially for families that had previously experienced poverty. Children had an 18% lower probability of having committed a minor crime. Labor force participation rates did not change as a result of the UBI.

Analysis of the Canadian Mincome project also found that labor force participation rates changed only slightly as a result of UBI payments. The study also found that hospitalizations declined for accidents, injuries and mental health. More children continued into grade 12. Another study of Mincome found that offering financial assistance to everyone regardless of their current income, wealth or employment does away with the moral consideration of who does and does not deserve help.

Finally, four large scale field experiments of basic income in the United States showed various positive results for children. In one state, attendance rates in grades 2 through 8 increased, teacher ratings of students rose, and test score improved. In another, significant reductions in dropouts from schools were found. In a third, the incidence of low birthweight rates declined in the most at-risk categories. In two of the studies home ownership was achieved more often by experimental families.

The Economic Hardship-Child Outcome Model

At the end of Chapter 2, we looked at the Family Stress Model. It posited a causal connection between socioeconomic status (SES) and stress within the family. As noted there, SES is usually based on three elements: income, education and job status. What the studies reviewed here demonstrate is that the first of these is primary. In the studies, there was no effort to modify the education or the type of job held by parents. The exception to this might be the employment and training requirements of the welfare reform experiments. However, you will recall that the projects that were focused solely on those requirements produced no effects. E&T programs are about getting a job, however limited and low paying, and usually about training programs rather than higher education. These findings suggest that the meaning of SES in this model should be limited to variations in income (and wealth). Indeed, in an earlier article that is precisely what two of the authors of the article discussed at the end of Chapter 2, the Congers, did.[104] They outlined a more specific model that included the following. *Economic hardship* (low income, high debt, low assets and negative financial events) leads to *economic pressure* (unmet material needs, unpaid debts and painful cutbacks). These in turn lead to *parent distress* (emotional and behavioral problems), which produces *disrupted family relations* (inter-parental conflict or withdrawal and harsh or inconsistent parenting). Finally, this produces *child and adolescent adjustment* (emotional problems, behavioral problems and impaired competence). In the studies I have reviewed, economic hardships were relieved in some way for experimental families leading to improved outcomes for families and children, but what should be remembered is that there was a continuation of economic hardship in all or some portion of the control families, in my reviewed studies, leading to the negative "child adjustments" that the Congers refer to. They also present the obverse of the stress model: the *Family Resource Model*. In that model the resources and the lack thereof are predicted to affect child outcomes. There are resources that are only indirectly related to finances but the critical ones such as health, education, housing, living arrangements, transportation, leisure activities, neighborhoods, safety, etc. are clearly produced or directly affected by income and wealth. I will refer to the combination of these as the *Economic Hardship-Child Outcome Model*.

Therefore, the studies presented support the Economic Hardship-Child Outcome model. Do the findings of these studies mean that traits and dispositions of family members are not important? Of course not, so long as those two terms are used to refer to individual differences in things like neurology, endocrinology, brain development, general health, to psychological traits like anger control, shyness, introversion-extroversion, parenting behaviors and to situations such

---

104 Rand Conger & Katherine Conger. (2008). Understanding the Processes through which Economic Hardship Influences Families and Children. Chapter 5 in *Handbook of Families and Poverty*, ed. Crane, D., & Heaton, T. Los Angeles: Sage Publications.

as, social isolation, quality of extended family relations and support, and so on. These play their part in the variations in responses of adults and children to economic hardship. However, such differences exist across all human beings at all social class levels.

I am not saying that money solves all problems, rather that lack of money, that is, economic hardship, exacerbates negative qualities, destructive behaviors and harmful human relationships while sufficient money makes the expression of positive qualities, supportive behaviors and beneficial relationships more likely. This might be called the *aggravation from deprivation-alleviation from relief* understanding. *Financial deprivation aggravates other problems in families and makes positive outcomes for children more unlikely while financial relief alleviates problems and makes positive outcomes more likely.*

Chapter 7

Contexts

So many proposals for relieving economic hardship seem to assume an unchanging national and world context. Solutions cannot be considered while pretending that we are living in 1980 or even in the year 2000. Major changes are taking place that have implications for how families and children might be helped. It may seem that we are veering rather far away from the topics considered in the previous chapters, but ways of addressing economic hardship of families only make sense when approached in this way. So, I ask that you bear with me in this chapter as we attempt to explain what is happening.

There are four critically important changing contexts that must be considered in selecting solutions to the problems of economic hardship: climate change, energy generation, income disparity and joblessness. Changing means just that: the social and economic context today is different from yesterday, and while the exact timing of future changes cannot be known, the features of the context tomorrow will be different from today. All four contexts are interrelated, however, and because of the dire consequences of a slow response to the first of these—climate change—rapid adaptation will be necessary to avoid disaster.

Changing Context 1: Climate Change

I know that this may seem like a real stretch to some readers. What does climate change have to do with improving the financial situation of families and children? There are two answers to that question.

First and most important, the changes that are occurring now and will continue into the near future have the potential to devastate world societies environmentally and economically. This includes the United

States. Environmental destruction will translate, and is translating right now, into economic destruction across our entire society from the rich to the poor. We describe this in the present section. Yet solutions to poverty, debt and family financial difficulties are often considered as if these changes are not happening. Here is a metaphor to illustrate what we are talking about.

You are *the* assistant director on a train tour. The train has many cars and passengers. It has operated well during the trip but now has climbed to a mountain top and is beginning its descent. The engineer just called you on your radio and informed you that the train's brakes appear to be failing and wants to know what he should do. You rush back to inform the tour director of the danger. He is talking to the tour doctor and cook. You describe the problem to him and tell him that this problem is critical and must be solved before the tour goes farther. He looks skeptical but agrees that it should be dealt with. However, he notes that there are other problems. He looks to the doctor who says that he has several people who somehow caught the flu, one individual with a violent allergic reaction to certain food, and he points to a woman in the same car who has an infection that needs to be treated with antibiotics. The cook says that families in the last few cars did not get breakfast and he needs to feed them. You point out that if the brakes fail this will become a runaway train that will certainly derail on the curves that are coming up. The director nods and says that he understands and will address the problem in order of priority. You wonder what could have a higher priority than derailing. The train begins to accelerate. Some of the passengers begin to look worried but the director refuses to become overly concerned for fear of panicking everyone…

This is a story of delay in addressing a dire threat in order to deal with other problems. Anyone who does not think that climate change brought on by global warming is the most important issue facing humanity today simply has not been paying attention. We all need to start paying attention.

A second answer regarding climate change and the economic wellbeing of families lies in the nature of the response needed. It must be rapid and comprehensive. The only response that makes sense at this late date is the full conversion of our electricity production from fossil fuels to renewables and abandonment of internal combustion engines and replacement with electrical. As we emphasize in the next section, the process of change is already occurring. It needs to be accelerated.

In 2025 there were 23 weather-related climate disasters that each cost $1 billion or more. "As of December 2025, the U.S. had sustained 426 such events with a total cost exceeding $3.1 trillion."[105] These dollar figures are large and hard to make personally relevant. Here is a more concrete way of thinking about it. There were about 133 million families in the U.S. in 2025. The weather disasters of a minimum $23 billion would amount to about $173 per family. But the cost of the total set of 426 events would amount to over $23,000 per family. The costs are mainly borne be families directly affected by each disaster, but they are also spread across the larger society in the form of government expenditures and higher insurance rates. Every indication is that destruction from climate disasters such as these will continue to increase. Now add to that cost other more subtle areas in which social debts are accruing due to climate change, such as changing patterns of disease, agricultural deterioration, destruction of forests, extended droughts in dryer regions, to name just a few. These will all exact an increasing financial toll in coming years.

We should note before describing this further that the primary reason why the US government has been so slow to address this problem is in large part due to the process that we describe in greater detail below: rent seeking. Large fossil fuel corporations have spent millions of dollars in the past 50 years supporting denialist think tanks, individuals posing as expert contrarians and politicians who have stood in the way of climate change solutions. Read this article by Ben Jervey, *How the Koch brothers got us here*, recounting the activities of only one fossil fuel corporation.[106] The Koch brothers spent years investing in colleges and universities, funding positions for faculty who were ideologically aligned with them. They spent millions funding think tanks and supporting politicians and various front groups to foster anti-global

---

105 Climate Central website. Available at: https://www.climatecentral.org/climate-services/billion-dollar-disasters

106 Ben Jervey. (2019). *How the Koch Brothers Got Us Here*. Bulletin of the Atomic Scientists. Available at: https://thebulletin.org/2019/09/how-the-koch-brothers-got-us-here/

warming ideas. They are not alone, of course. The corporate boards and CEOs of several of the large fossil fuel companies are implicated. They have engaged in such behavior because they realize that awareness of the problem and remedial actions could hurt their short-term bottom line, the returns available to shareholders and the value of their stock. Never mind the long-term harm to the environment and to society, which economists call *externalities*. Externalities can be negative or positive. The negative kinds in this case are the costs to us all resulting from burning fossil fuels that everyone in society must pay for, over and above the monetary cost of the product. For example, $3.00 a gallon for gasoline does not begin to cover the costs to society resulting from the excess CO_2 emitted in extracting it from crude oil and as it is combusted in an engine. By continuing along this path these companies are in effect treating environmental devastation and large-scale deaths of human beings as something that can simply be ignored. Such negative externalities cost the company *nothing*, but they may have massive economic and health consequences for the rest of society and for future generations. The thing that is most difficult to believe, however, is their obliviousness to the coming destruction of their own enterprises, as we also consider in the next section.

At this late date, virtually no professional among the many thousands working in climatology or closely related areas such as oceanography and glaciology denies the existence and causes of global warming and climate change. Contrarians that remain in the field of climatology proper are few, and even they now qualify their denials in various ways. So, I will not spend time attempting to counter the many specious contrarian arguments that have been presented over the past several decades. The best source for *refutations based on science* is the "climate change myths" section of the Skeptical Science website.[107]

The physics of global warming is well established. One of the first exercises that students do in Climatology 101, is to estimate the average temperature of the earth by treating it as a black body disc exposed to the full range of solar radiation but with an atmosphere composed of oxygen and nitrogen only. Those two gases are essentially transparent to electromagnetic radiation, including infrared light. What would the

---

107   Available at: https://skepticalscience.com/argument.php

earth's temperature be if our atmosphere contained no carbon dioxide (CO2), methane, nitrous oxide or other greenhouse gases at all? It turns out that with no greenhouse gases the earth's average temperature would be about 0 degrees Fahrenheit (or in Celsius, 18 degrees below zero) versus the present average temp of 59 degrees Fahrenheit. There would be little or no water vapor, which is also a potent greenhouse gas, in the atmosphere because it would be too cold. The earth would be a snowball. Thus, CO2 in tiny amounts is critical for a livable earth. However, complex human societies developed with CO2-equivalent levels in the range of 250 to 300 parts per million (ppm), a tiny amount but just about right for temperate and human-friendly temperatures in many parts of the world. As of this writing, CO2 levels worldwide have increased to 420 ppm and beyond. This is higher than at any level in human history. We know this because paleo-climatologists who specialize in climate history have measured such levels in atmospheric gases trapped in yearly layers of ice cores drawn in Greenland and Antarctica as well as using other more indirect methods.

I say, *"we"* have increased these levels, because it has been established beyond a doubt that the higher levels of greenhouse gases have arisen from combustion of coal, oil and natural gas during the past 200 years. We know this through studies of increased levels of certain carbon isotopes in our atmosphere that are associated with buried oil and coal, something again that no competent scientist disputes. Warming is occurring and human activity is the cause. The average temperature of the earth has increased during this period by about 1.27O C (2.29O F) in 2020 with the largest increases occurring in the past 40 years.[108] Greenhouse gas increase is the only plausible explanation for this warming, and we are already experiencing the disastrous consequences.

Readers may remember the outcry from climate deniers in the early 2000's that 1998 was the hottest year on record and the years following were actually cooler. "Global warming has paused," they said. Then came 2005, which was hotter than 1998 and later 2009 which was hotter still. The clamor slowed and then stopped—by everyone except the most foolish naysayers—as several individual years from 2010 to 2025 have now been shown to be warmer. There was no pause in global warming. It is continuing and increasing.

---

108   See https://climatechangetracker.org/global-warming/yearly-average-temperature

Over 90% of the additional heat being trapped goes into the oceans while the remainder is absorbed by land. The earth's average atmospheric surface temperature continues to increase but has varied from year-to-year dependent in part on the El Nino-La Nina cycles in the Pacific Ocean as warmer waters either turned over releasing heat into the atmosphere or remained deep down heating the surface air less. Rapidly increasing ocean warming has now been confirmed in multiple empirical studies.[109] Sea ice is melting all over the world leading to further increases in ocean temperatures as dark waters, which absorb more sunlight, replace white reflective ice. This has significant implications for the welfare of human beings, including parents and their children. Change in the cryosphere is reported by a large body of climate scientists.[110] These include more rapid sea level rise, increased coastal erosion, and the intensification of hurricanes resulting in worsening floods. Warmer waters and increased atmospheric water vapor lead to more intense and slower moving, sometimes stalled, hurricanes. Rising sea levels result in higher storm surges and increased flooding during storms. Jeff Goodell's book *The Water Will Come: Rising Seas, Sinking Cities, and the Remaking of the Civilized World* describes well what is already happening and will occur shortly.[111] Goodbye, Miami and New Orleans. And if we do not act now to prevent it, then slightly further down the road Manhattan, Houston and other similar coastal locales will be overcome. What this means is that millions of families in the United States and all around the world will have to relocate from low-lying coastal areas in the next 10 to 30 years. The economic consequences are going to be enormous even if we do something now. If we do nothing they will be catastrophic. I wrote a fiction book on this topic that describes the resulting migration.[112]

A number of recent studies have examined the melting that is going on in Antarctica. The land glaciers that make up the West

---

109 For instance, look at: https://yaleclimateconnections.org/2026/01/2025-was-earths-3rd-warmest-year-on-record/

110 See: https://www.ipcc.ch/srocc/

111 Jeff Goodell. (2017). *The Water Will Come: Rising Seas, Sinking Cities, and the Remaking of the Civilized World.* New York: Little, Brown and Company.

112 L. Anthony Loman. (2025). *"Striving, Zooming Children: A SciFi, CliFi, AiFi Novel.* See: https://www.amazon.com/Striving-Zooming-Kids-Sci-Fi-Cli-Fi-ebook/dp/B0G4NTSWBH/ref=sr_1_1?crid=1HPQD0WWWJOSW&dib=eyJ2IjoiMSJ9.____21h_ahfGrtcbWDjFF3ddfw.-dyAup0yFQhMB_1FhEVZKAUzSx3gNjuHieT0hVQxJuw&dib_tag=se&keywords=striving%2C+zooming+kids&qid=1769799277&sprefix=Striving+z%2Caps%2C188&sr=8-1

Antarctic Ice Sheet (WAIS) are moving inexorably into the ocean. This is abetted by the melting of the ice shelves that extend out over the ocean. The shelves have previously slowed and blocked the flow of land ice into the ocean. But now the shelves are being eroded underneath by changes in wind and sea currents brought on by climatic changes in the Pacific Ocean.[113] When WAIS finally flows into the sea, sea levels will rise by 10 feet worldwide. We have been told by popular science writers that this is not imminent. However, climate science, like all science, is inherently conservative.

I could go on looking at the ongoing effects of global warming and future projections of climate changes but will stop here. A good general source for fuller information is the 2023 Synthesis Report of the Intergovernmental Panel on Climate Change (IPCC).[114] The predicted warming above 2°C will eventually result in the deaths of many millions, even billions, of human beings, not to mention members of other species. We need to think not just about the effects on families and children today but about our descendants. Take time to read Elizabeth Kolbert's *The Sixth Great Extinction* to get a sense of this.[115]

Changing Context 2: The End of Fossil Fuels and the Green New Deal

Another change is occurring that is related to the previous discussion. Some of the worst consequences of global warming may be avoided but only if the transition from fossil fuels to renewables in energy production and transportation is accelerated. That transition is already happening, but we need to make it happen faster. The abandonment of fossil fuels will have negative consequences for the world economy in the short term. However, there is a potential bright side to the change as we try to demonstrate: a rapid transition to renewables will create millions of jobs, many of which will be available to currently struggling middle class and working-class parents and to those currently living in poverty.

---

113 Adrian Jenkins, Deb Shoosmith, Pierre Dutrieux, Stan Jacobs, Tae Wan Kim, Sang Hoon Lee, Ho Kyung Ha & Sharon Stammerjohn. (2018). West Antarctic Ice Sheet retreat in the Amundsen Sea driven by decadal oceanic variability. *Nature Geoscience, 11,* 733-38. Eric Rignot, Jeremie Mouginot, Bernd Scheuchl, Michiel van den Broeke, Melchior van Wessem & and Mathieu Morlighem. (2019). Four decades of Antarctic Ice Sheet mass balance from 1979–2017. PNAS 116 (4) 1095-1103.

114 Go to https://www.ipcc.ch/report/sixth-assessment-report-cycle/

115 Elizabeth Kolbert. (2014). *The Sixth Great Extinction.* New York: Henry Holt.

The costs of producing electricity using wind, solar and storage (WSS) technologies have been decreasing rapidly during the past 30 years. That trend is projected to continue. Clean Energy Portfolios (CEP) powerplants are cheaper to install and maintain than new gas-fired power plants. Gas-fired power plants in the US have a projected cost of $48 to $109 per MWh, as compared to $39 to $78 for solar plants. It is clear that construction of new gas plants are boondoggles that, if built, will turn into stranded assets. Stranded assets are those that must be abandoned before capital costs can be recovered. It will simply be too expensive and thus uncompetitive to generate power using natural gas. Natural gas must be purchased for the entire lifetime of gas-fired plants, even after all capital costs have been recovered. Natural gas costs money. The sun and wind are essentially free. This was predicted in an older Rocky Mountain Institute (RMI) report that presented the shift to CEPs as an economic opportunity rather than some form of governmental imposition.[116]

A great deal has been written about the end of coal and petroleum production. It is coming, but there still appears to be debate concerning whether the transition will be (or can be) rapid or slow. A rapid transition would be good for the environment and for the long-term welfare of families and children. The energy transition process is outlined clearly in World Economic Forum (WEF) white paper, *Fostering Effective Energy Transition 2025*.[117]

CEOs of fossil fuel companies are unable to face reality. A blunt essay a decade ago by Irina Slav, *Diversify or Die, Big Oil's Dwindling Options for Survival* on the Oil Price website suggested that big oil companies should begin investing in renewables. She pointed to one example, the large company, French Total, which before her writing in 2016 had invested $1.1 billion in power storage systems. She asserted that other oil giants had better follow suit.[118] Phillips 66, Lukoil, Chevron, ExxonMobil, British Petroleum and a myriad of other

---

116 Charles Teplin, Mark Dyson, Alex Engle, & Grant Glazor. (2019). *The Growing Market for Clean Energy Portfolios: Economic Opportunities for a Shift from New Gas-Fired Generation to Clean Energy across the United States Electricity Industry.* Rocky Mountain Institute. Available at: https://rmi.org/insight/clean-energy-portfolios-pipelines-and-plants/

117 This can be found online at: https://www.weforum.org/publications/fostering-effective-energy-transition-2025/in-full/

118 Irina Slav. (2016). Diversify of Die? Big Oil's Dwindling Options for Survival. Oil Price. Available at: https://oilprice.com/Energy/Energy-General/Diversify-Or-Die-Big-Oils-Dwindling-Options-For-Survival.html

companies need to stop their senseless climate change denial and follow along with investments and acquisitions not only in energy storage but in wind and solar electricity (and other renewable) generation.

An analyst with an impressive record of accurate forecasting regarding technological change is in basic agreement with this assessment. This is Jeremy Rifkin in his book, *The Green New Deal: Why the Fossil Fuel Civilization will Collapse by 2028 and the Bold Economic Plan to Save Life on Earth*.[119] If you read no other book on addressing climate change read this one. It is clear, concise and most importantly Rifkin offers practical steps. Rather than wringing hands and crying, his message is let's get to work and here is a way we can do it. I note here, however, that Rifkin's dating concerning the demise of fossil fuel electricity by 2028 may be overly optimistic.

Solar, wind, and other renewable resources in the United States generated 24.2%% of electrical energy in 2024.[120] Solar and wind generation have been accelerating, and we can expect this to continue to rise in the US and other developed countries. Renewables in the European Union rose from 17.5% in 2017 to 25 percent in 2023 and continue to increase.

Both RMI and Rifkin advocate various policy initiatives to speed the transition from coal and natural gas generation of electricity to solar and wind. Rifkin lists 23 key initiatives that will be necessary.[121]

My list concerns some of the changes that will be necessary in the move to full wind, solar and storage (WSS) tech. This means a reworking of the energy, transportation and logistics infrastructure. A massive federal-state-local government plan is needed that may involve in part various Public Service Employment (PSE) jobs funded by government but will largely involve private enterprise jobs supported through tax incentives, new laws and regulations, and financing from both public and private sources.

---

119 Jeremy Rifkin. (2019). *The Green New Deal: Why the Fossil Fuel Civilization will Collapse by 2028 and the Bold Economic Plan to Save Life on Earth*. New York: St. Martin's Press.
120 Available at: https://electrek.co/2025/02/27/renewables-generated-24-percent-us-electricity-2024-eia-data/
121 Ibid, p. 222ff.

Concerning public versus private control, virtually all analysts and commentators, both conservatives and progressives, agree on the need for government involvement and control in upgrading and changing our infrastructure. Even the most libertarian thinkers know that large scale and rapid infrastructure change cannot be accomplished through private enterprise alone but must involve citizens and government. Infrastructure is produced and controlled by entire communities for the benefit and protection of all citizens and social groups. In this way the Green New Deal can become a uniting force in American society bringing together citizens of diverse backgrounds and political orientations.

There are many examples of past successful government sponsored infrastructure projects that made the United States the world leader in developing what Rifkin calls the *Second Industrial Revolution* infrastructure. The Tennessee Valley Authority (TVA) project under President Roosevelt in the 1930s, decried by some at the time as a massive mistake, was instead a major success bringing affordable electricity to hundreds of thousands of families in the South while controlling flooding and initiating reforesting of stripped lands. Another example is the Rural Electrification Act of 1936 that provided loans to bring electricity to remote rural areas through the creation of rural electric cooperatives over the following 15 years. Local groups planned and controlled the process under these laws. Most of the co-ops that were created still exist today and function as citizen-controlled infrastructure agencies. The best model for scale might be the Federal-Aid Highway Act of 1956 which produced the 40,000+ mile long interstate highway system over the entire continental US within a couple of decades. This was a combined federal, state and local public-private effort stimulated and financed by the federal government. Taxpayer money was used for most of the construction. Incidentally, it was financed through imposition of a carbon tax through a small increase in the tax on gasoline. We need this kind of effort again, except this time on an even more massive scale and an accelerated timetable. If done, this can provide well-paying jobs for millions of workers with the consequential benefits to families with children. Here are some of the more important elements:

Installation of solar and wind by consumers and businesses into distributed power generation systems. This will include the creation of energy microgrids. A microgrid is a grouping of energy generation and storage at the local level. The generation will be largely from solar but also from small scale wind, small in-stream hydro generation, and from biomass sources. One of the best references to read for clearly explained, and brief, descriptions of various components of microgrids and other systems is: ***Drawdown: The Most Comprehensive Plan Ever Produced to Reverse Global Warming.***[122] Distributed systems involve collections of micro-grids that can function independently of one another or can join and share power. The ability to function independently would guard against large scale failure and extended power outages. Modern economies simply cannot function without a regular and reliable source of electric power. Recent examples of electrical blackouts lasting days or weeks because of wildfires and floods illustrate the ongoing dangers of the current highly centralized macro grid system. Tax incentives can be offered at the federal and state level to stimulate the changes, but direct government funding would also be needed. In addition, laws and regulations will be required to insure that consumers who produce power (prosumers) are compensated fairly for the electricity at market prices.

Installation of the elements of a smart grid to feed generation and usage information to and from the larger grid. Current macro grid systems utilize one-way communication. Smart grids will involve two-way communication permitting efficient use of the kind of distributed power embodied in microgrids. Those currently generating electricity at their home or business and feeding back into the electrical grid will already be familiar with smart meters that mediate, record and transmit information on electricity usage and production back into the system. Internet-of-Things (IOT) devices will include smart thermostats, web-connected electricity plugs and instruments to monitor and regulate appliances, lighting and other electrical devices within homes and businesses. Two-way communication between consumers and producers will make the use of electricity significantly more efficient.[123]

---

122   Paul Harkin (editor). (2017). Drawdown: *The Most Comprehensive Plan ever Produced to Reverse Global Warming.* New York: Penguin Random House, LLC.

123   Ibid. page 209.

Retrofitting of all buildings to energy efficiency standards. By "all" we mean each of the 127 million plus houses in the US and the nearly 6 million commercial buildings that are not already energy efficient. This will be a massive restoration necessary for efficient and less wasteful use of power. Building regulations will be instituted that require new construction to be sufficiently insulated and sealed to retain heat in the winter and remain cool in the summer. Passive solar designs of new homes and businesses will be favored. Retrofitting will also be partially financed through tax deduction but also may involve grants at various government levels.

Enhancement of high voltage transmission lines to carry electricity from sparsely populated areas, where large solar and wind farms may be located, to large urban areas that are unable to generate sufficient electricity on their own. Again, this will require upgrades, redundancies and large-scale electrical storage. Lines will be equipped with sensors that will permit information on usage to be monitored and reported in both directions.

Tax incentives to stimulate the purchase of all electric vehicles. This may also include hydrogen fuel cell vehicles. Laws should be written restricting the use of internal combustion vehicles in urban areas, as is already happening in other countries around the world. Current tax rebates supporting purchases of electric cars and trucks should be continued and expanded. Installation of electric vehicle recharging stations will be promoted nationwide. Another source of work may be installation of hydrogen storage facilities for fuel cell vehicles.

Upgrading public broadband Wi-Fi to increase speed and extension. The US currently lags behind most developed and many developing nations in this regard. This will enhance the functionality of the smart grid.

A word should also be said concerning an objection to this that is sometimes heard. It is that the US is already becoming more energy efficient and greener, and that the problem is Third World and developing countries, which are lagging behind. We are indeed producing less CO2 in generating electricity due to the shift from coal to natural gas. The idea seems to be that unless these poorer countries change first, upgrading in the US will be both useless and unfair. The exact opposite is true. Compared to Europe, South Korea and China, the US has been slow in making changes and is being left behind. We will come to regret this in the next few years if we do not get on board. On the other hand, if Americans move forward aggressively with a Green New Deal, the rest of the world that is not already ahead of us will follow. Everyone around the world followed and imitated us as we built a nationwide electricity and transportation system in the 20th Century. We need to lead the world again.

Changing Context 3: Income and Wealth Disparity or Welfare for the Rich

In this section the disparity in incomes in the U.S. is considered. It is increasing. *Welfare for the upper income tier* exists and has increased in recent years.

It is hard to avoid literature describing rising income disparity. The Gini (G) coefficient is often cited. This is a measure of inequality in incomes in various states, provinces and nations. The methods of calculating G are described in various references.[124] It ranges in decimal values from zero to one. If we convert it to a percentage ranging from 0 to 100, it makes more sense to most people. A nation or state with a G of 100% would be one in which one individual had all the income and everyone else had no income. A G of 0% would mean that everyone had equal incomes, a perfectly equal share of the income of the nation. So, a lower score means greater equality of income while a higher score indicates greater disparity.

Generally, countries range from about 20 to 50 on the index. According to the World Population Review, the U.S. ranked high in disparity among developed countries with a 2026 score of 41.8%. Compare this to Canada (29.9%), the United Kingdom (32.4%), France (31.2%), Germany (32.4%), Netherlands (25,7%) and Sweden (31.6%). The U.S. score in the 40's is comparable to that of some of the poorer countries in Africa and Central America.[125] The U.S.

---

124 The Wikipedia article describes it well: https://en.wikipedia.org/wiki/Gini_coefficient

125 World Population Review: Gini Coefficient by Country 2019. Available at: http://worldpopulationreview.com/countries/gini-coefficient-by-country/

Census Bureau computes Gini scores as well. Except for comparative purposes, G is rather opaque. The distribution of U.S. national income by quintiles, the population divided into five equal groups by income, gives a better idea of changing disparity. In 1970, the share of income from lowest to highest quintile was: 4.1%, 10.8%, 17.4%, 24.5% and 43.3%. In 2000, the figures were: 3.6%, 8.9%, 14.8%, 23.0% and 49.8%. In 2024, they were 3.1%, 8.2%, 13.9%, 22.6%, 52.2%. Over this period, the highest quintile's share increased by 8.9%, while the combined share of the three lowest quintiles declined by 7.3%.[126] This illustrates the declining fortunes during the past 60+ years of the *precariat*, Guy Standing's term, mentioned earlier, for the economically vulnerable portion of modern populations. The changes shown in these states depict increase in financial distress and the shrinkage of the U.S. middle class. The richest part of the population has acquired more and more of the nation's total income over this period.

Income refers to money received during a given year. Wealth refers to accumulation of assets. I was referring to one element of wealth in Chapter 1 when considering savings of American families. For instance, a person or family may have an annual income that permits them to survive but very little or zero wealth. Wealth includes cash savings combined with other assets, such as stocks and bonds, property and other material possessions. Looking at 2024 data, the top 1% of households possess 30.45% of the total wealth while the bottom 50% hold 2.5%.[127]

The reaction of some to these disparities in income and wealth is, so what? The important thing is that the whole society is richer, isn't it? You might think that. Compare the situation and possessions of the average working-class individual in a developed society like the U.S. to that of a similarly situated person 200 years ago or to a lower-class family today in India. You might simply dismiss income and wealth inequality as a problem until you begin to examine the studies of its effects across entire societies. In general, great disparity is associated with a plethora of social and health problems and, particularly in

---

126 Statista: https://www.statista.com/statistics/203247/shares-of-household-income-of-quintiles-in-the-us/

127 Wealth inequality in the United States: https://en.wikipedia.org/wiki/Wealth_inequality_in_the_United_States

developed societies, high costs of addressing those problems. A book published some years ago by Richard Wilkinson and Kate Pickett, *The Spirit Level: Why Greater Equality Makes Societies Stronger* considers these issues. It is a tour-de-force of comparative analyses showing the relationship between income inequality and various negative societal and state-level outcomes. A more recent book by the same two authors is *The Inner Level: How more Equal Societies Reduce Stress, Restore Sanity and Improve Everyone's Well-Being*, in which they discuss more fully the effects of relative deprivation on mental and physical well-being.[128]

Comparisons among developed nations and among US states that vary in income inequality are striking. As inequality increases, the level of problems in various areas rises. The United States has the most extreme inequality among developed countries and the worse outcomes. Here are two that were considered in Chapter 3 and are relevant to child welfare and development.

The greater the inequality, the higher the rate of infant mortality. For example, among OECD countries, the United States ranked 60 highest with a rate of 7.3 deaths per 1,000 live births in 2024. Thus 59 other OECD countries ranked lower! The rate goes down in countries with decreasing levels of income inequality. For example, in Japan and Norway the infant mortality rates were 1.9 & 1.8/1000.[129]

The greater the inequality, the lower youth scores are on tests of math and literacy. Among OECD countries in 2022 the U.S. ranked 20 on the Programme for International Students Assessment (PISA) scores in mathematics, with generally higher scores in countries with lower inequality.[130]

Wilkinson and Pickett also show that health outcomes such as life expectancy, obesity, mental illness and use of drugs are worse in countries with greater income disparity. The U.S. is comparatively

---

128 Richard Wilkinson & Kate Pickett. (2009). *The Sprit Level: Why Greater Equality Makes Societies Stronger.* New York: Bloomsbury Press. Richard Wilkinson & Kate Pickett. (2018). *The Inner Level: How more Equal Societies Reduce Stress, Restore Sanity and Improve Everyone's Well-Being.* New York: Penguin Press.

129 Country comparison tables are available at: https://worldpopulationreview.com/country-rankings/infant-mortality-rate-by-country

130 OECD PISA: Results in Focus (2022). The report is available at: https://www.oecd.org/en/publications/pisa-2022-results-volume-i_53f23881-en.html

worse off in each of these areas compared to other countries with lower income disparity. In addition, U.S. states also vary substantially in income inequality and the same differences in various social, biological and health outcomes are correlated as well. Another outcome is poorer educational attainment in U.S. states with greater income inequality.

In explaining these findings some have emphasized the importance of individual psychological effects that come from each person comparing his or her level of income and wealth—or more generally socioeconomic status—with others in society. It is true that there are studies showing that poorer people suffer feelings of low self-worth and shame associated with their lower status. This occurs in poor underdeveloped countries, but it is also observed in developing and highly developed societies, even though lower income groups in developed countries may be substantially better off than their counterparts in less developed nations.[131] However, my experience and observation of the situation of many families in studies conducted with my colleagues have convinced me that *absolute deprivation* of families and children continues to be a problem, even for families in developed countries and particularly in the United States. Look back at what was presented earlier about these families: unhealthy and unsafe housing, homelessness, not enough food and food variety, inadequate clothing, inadequate transportation, inability to pay for utilities, inability to pay for emergency expenses like health care, and many others. Note that the risk of debt and inadequate savings are real problems for many working-class and middle-class families in the precariat as much as for the very poor. It is true that feelings of low self-worth are in people's heads, but that does not mean that the material needs that engender their feelings are not real.

Significant and growing disparities in income exist today in the United States. The rich are getting richer and most of the rest of the population are getting poorer. Income disparity is growing and families with children are being hurt. Why is this happening? One answer is that manipulation of public policy has occurred, particularly in the past 50 years, by wealthy individuals and representatives of

---

131　For example: Robert Walker, Grace Bantebya Kyomuhendo, Elaine Chase & Sohail Choudhry. (2013). Poverty in Global Perspective: Is Shame a Common Denominator? *Journal of Social Policy* 42, 2, 215-33.

large corporations that provides economic advantages to them and consequently disadvantages to the rest of the population.

The shift of money that we have seen from the lower income groups to the highest income group has been accomplished in large part by what economists call *rent-seeking or rentierism*. Rent-seeking is a political process through which laws and regulations are written to direct free cash to powerful companies and individuals. Or, as defined in Wikipedia: rent-seeking is that act of growing one's existing wealth by manipulating public policy or economic conditions without creating new wealth.[132] A clearly written piece on this by Rutger Bregman was published in the Guardian newspaper. It was entitled: *No, Money is not created at the Top. It is Merely Devoured There.*[133] As Bregman says, the rentier is someone who uses their control over something that already exists in order to increase their own wealth. In other words, they are in fact taking rather than making. Another lengthy treatise is the book *The Price of Inequality: How Today's Divided Society Endangers our Future* by Joseph Stiglitz.[134] Another detailed source for understanding rentierism worldwide is Guy Standing's book The Corruption of Capitalism.[135]

I note here that writings by economists often present much more complex and multivariate explanations of the inequality that is happening. For example, James Galbraith, in his book *Inequality, What Everyone Needs to Know,* presented a long discussion spanning two chapters on the causes of inequality in the United States and in the World as a whole.[136] He discussed the roles of technology, education, minimum wage, immigration, trade unions, government itself, different types of political systems, violence, revolutions, increase in the control of banks (so called, 'financialization'), oil booms and shocks, debt, and other causes in fostering inequality. I am not denying that such causes

---

132 Available at: https://en.wikipedia.org/wiki/Rent-seeking

133 Rutger Bregman. (2017). No, Money is not created at the Top. It is Merely Devoured There. The Guardian, Opinion Money, March 30, 2017. Available at: https://www.theguardian.com/commentisfree/2017/mar/30/wealth-banks-google-facebook-society-economy-parasites

134 Joseph Stiglitz. (2012). *The Price of Inequality: How Today's Divided Society Endangers our Future. New York: W.W. Norton & Co.*

135 Guy Standing. (2016). *The Corruption of Capitalism: Why Rentiers Thrive and Work Does Not Pay.* London: Biteback Publishing Ltd.

136 James K. Galbraith. (2016). Inequality: What Everyone Needs to Know. New York: Oxford University Press. The sections in the book referred to are Chapter 6 "Causes of changing inequality in the United States" and Chapter 7 "Causes of changing inequality in the world," pages 71-111, where he speculates on such matters.

exist. For example, in the next section I show that technological change has led to the disappearance of jobs for individuals without a higher education. That can be assumed to contribute to income inequality arising from joblessness and poor paying jobs. The concern here is a central cause of the ongoing and accelerating *process* of shifting money into the pockets of already wealthy individuals and corporations that is occurring regardless of the many more general causes that economists point out.

It should be noted that so-called free markets can only work when laws and regulations are in place that govern the definitions of property, ownership, the essential components of contracts, the conditions necessary for bankruptcies, constraints on monopolies, the length of patents, and a myriad of related issues, along with the enforcement of the defining laws and the regulations accompanying them. There are no free markets in the absence of these, as Robert Reich clearly and convincingly outlines in his book *Saving Capitalism: For the Many not the Few.*[137] Free markets require governance. No governance equals market chaos. Rent-seeking occurs when the laws and regulations meant to define, control and ensure balance, fairness and most importantly *competition* in markets are either suppressed or modified in various ways to move income to a select few. Here are some examples of laws and policies enacted in the past few decades responsible for shifting money away from the majority of the population and into the pockets of already wealthy corporations and individuals.

Welfare for Bankers. The bailout after the financial crisis called the Great Recession consisted of a transfer of billions of dollars to the banks and bankers who had caused the crisis. This was done with little or no penalties applied to the wrongdoers. Not surprisingly this also led to the inordinate enrichment of many individuals at the top of the banking profession, at the expense of the rest of society—a *welfare transfer* from the middle class to the rich. But worse and perhaps more debilitating are the continuing cash transfers embodied in zero and negative interest loans to banks. As Bregman notes, this leads to high levels of debt throughout society (and in fact worldwide) as bankers push loans and get essentially free returns in the form of interest,

---

137   Robert Reich. (2015). *Saving Capitalism: For the Many not the Few.* New York: Vintage Books.

commissions, brokerage fees, and more. This amounts to billions of dollars in free money to this class, the rent that economists talk about. Yes, their employees work hard but the banks have essentially pilfered wealth rather than producing it themselves. Read the references in Bregman's article for a more complete analysis of the debt problem.

Welfare for Pharmaceutical Companies. Why are the prices for the same medication so much higher in the United States compared to European nations and even in neighboring Canada? The answer is rent-seeking. Again, hundreds of Washington lobbyists and millions of dollars in political contributions have kept US politicians from enacting price controls on pharmaceuticals like those in Europe and Canada. This along with changes in patent laws that insure longer exclusive ownership of drugs and medications before they become generic has led to billions of dollars transferred from the pockets of ordinary citizens into the coffers of the corporations and their shareholders.

Welfare through Corporate Avoidance of Taxes. The most blatant form of rent-seeking is low tax rates and various tax loopholes for corporations and individuals with large incomes. At least 55 of the largest corporation in the United States paid zero taxes in 2020. Their pretax income amounted to $40.5 billion.[138] However, this is just one example of what has been developing over the past 60 years as tax laws have been modified. If large companies and wealthy individuals avoid paying taxes but ordinary working class and middle-class families do pay taxes, then avoidance of taxes represents a welfare gift from lower income to higher income groups.

Welfare for Investors: Capital gains. Under 2025 tax law, the long-term rates (on assets held longer than one year) were 0% for incomes of $48,350 or less. On incomes above this up to $533,400 the rate was 15% for single filers. Over this amount the rate was 20%.[139] The large part of asset purchases, like stocks, bonds and property, are made by people in the top of the income pyramid. Of the benefits of low capital gains taxes, 77.8% were received by the top 1% of incomes and another 12.2% went to the next 4% for a total of 90% to the richest

---

138   ITEP article available at: https://itep.org/55-profitable-corporations-zero-corporate-tax/
139   Available at: https://www.kiplinger.com/taxes/new-irs-long-term-capital-gains-tax-thresholds

5% of Americans in 2019.[140] This is another example of tax policies that benefit a tiny segment of American Society.[141]

Many other examples can be found in Guy Standing's book, cited above, which as we note is one of the best analyses of the process of creating and maintaining rentier economies.[142] Standing shows how subsidies to asset holders have increased worldwide in the past few decades. Subsidies for land, property, mineral rights, intellectual property and financial assets are all forms of rental income that have nothing to do with "hard work" or production but are simply handouts to rentiers. He cites examples of lower tax rates for wealthy individuals and corporations, lack of government action regarding tax avoidance and evasion and direct subsidies in various forms.

Standing also describes the bank bailouts during the Great Recession as examples of "rent for failure" and how the benefits to banks have continued through availability of "cheap money."[143] He presents sundry examples of "patent trolling and hoovering" permitted to wealthy corporation, like the previous example of extended patents for pharmaceutical companies.[144] Other examples can be found in the aforementioned book by Joseph Stiglitz. Stiglitz was focused on the United States. He analyzes how macroeconomic policy and a central bank have enriched the 1% in this country. A priority in reversing this is curbing excesses at the top by restricting the leverage and liquidity of banks, making banks and credit card companies more competitive, curbing bonuses that encourage risk taking and closing offshore banking centers. The latter is nothing more than a mechanism to realize tax evasion and avoidance.[145]

Democracy has been perverted in this process. The perversion consists of excess political power achieved by funneling back to

---

140 Steve Wahhoff. (2019). *Capital Gains Tax Breaks are Finally on the Defensive.* Article on the Institute on Taxation and Economic Policy. Available at: https://itep.org/capital-gains-tax-breaks-are-finally-on-the-defensive/

141 For a full description of this and sensible solutions that would benefit our society, read: William Rice & Frank Clemente. (2019). *Fair Taxes Now: Revenue Options for a Fair Tax System.* Americans for Tax Fairness. Available at: https://americansfortaxfairness.org/wp-content/uploads/ATF-Fair-Taxes-Now-Report-FINAL-FINAL-4-12-19.pdf

142 Guy Standing. (2016). *The Corruption of Capitalism: Why Rentiers Thrive and Work Does Not Pay.* London: Biteback Publishing Ltd.

143 Ibid. pp. 114-26.

144 Ibid. pp. 49ff.

145 Joseph Stiglitz, *The Price of Inequality*, op. cit. pp. 269-70.

politicians a portion of the billions of dollars bestowed on the rich. There are makers and takers at all levels of society but the imbalance of "taking" at the top has reached a crisis level and needs to be redressed.

There is also the question of appearances. If you have ever looked at political cartoons from around 1900 you will be familiar with images of corpulent men smoking cigars and sitting on piles of cash. To avoid the response to greedy capitalists and monopolies during that period, current rentiers know that they must present themselves in a positive light. They are well dressed and affable. The present-day media aids and abets this by naïve acceptance of the underlying stereotypes embodied in "trickledown" and "supply side" economics that support this image of those at the top as the "makers," the producers, the hard workers. This supports the idea that extra money channeled to them will lead to beneficial effects for everyone. Those further down the income scale are implicitly or explicitly pictured as "takers" standing with their hands out. Yet, the evidence is that rather than helping society generally the laws and regulations promoting rent-seeking have harmed the large majority of the population as wages have stagnated or grown only marginally over the past 50 to 60 years and as the bottom 80% of families have gotten poorer while the top 20% and especially the top 5% have gotten richer. For a recent and highly detailed history of this, read Binyamin Appelbaum's *The Economists' Hour: How the False Prophets of Free Markets Fractured Our Society*.[146] When confronted with neoliberal supply-side justifications for policies, we each need to ask for evidence that they have worked up to now. They have not. Think about this the next time you see a fabulously wealthy individual prattling on cable news.

As Bregman says, it does not have to be this way. "Toll gates can be torn down, financial products can be banned, tax havens dismantled, lobbies tamed, and patents rejected. Higher taxes on the ultra-rich can make rentierism less attractive, precisely because society's biggest freeloaders are at the very top of the pyramid. And we can more fairly distribute our earnings on land, oil, and innovation through a system of, say, employee shares, or a universal basic income."[147]

---

146 Binyamin Appelbaum. (2019). *The Economists' Hour: How the False Prophets of Free Markets Fractured Our Society*. New York: Little, Brown and Company.

147 Rutger Bregman. (2017). *No, Money is not created at the Top. It is Merely Devoured There*. The Guardian, Opinion Money, March 30, 2017. Available at: https://www.theguardian.com/commentisfree/2017/mar/30/wealth-banks-google-facebook-society-economy-parasites

Changing Context 4: Jobs and Joblessness

The following is a consideration of longer-term change, although it has already begun. It has implications for the title of this book which includes the word *money*. If most jobs disappear in the future and much of what people and families need becomes essentially free, then money might simply become superfluous.

This changing context is related to the first two discussed in that the rapid transition necessary in the energy infrastructure and in transportation will require many new jobs. So, in the short term at least, necessary and meaningful employment can be created as we replace gas and coal electricity generation with renewables, as we upgrade our infrastructure generally, and as gas vehicles are replaced with electrical and fuel cell cars and trucks. However, I am not arguing that a Green New Deal will lead to *full employment*. Full employment has been strongly advocated by authors and analysts across the political spectrum from conservative to liberal for many years. In fact, I am not sure that full employment at this point in our technological development is a good thing, if the term refers purely to wage and salary jobs, as we note further on in our discussion of the value of "women's work."

More and more jobs are being taken over by automation, robotics, artificial intelligence and the digitization of commerce (Ecommerce). The debate about this is ongoing with some analysts insisting that productivity will increase dramatically in the next two to three decades and fewer and fewer human workers will be needed while others follow the traditional line advocated by economists over the past 100 years that tech changes destroy some jobs but eventually create a surplus of new kinds of jobs that replace those that were lost. For example, technology destroyed farm jobs at the turn of the twentieth century but new technology resulted in factory jobs to replace them.

The elephant in the room in these analyses is climate change, which, if not addressed, will make many of the much vaunted beneficial tech advances moot as society is overwhelmed by one disaster after another.

In 2013, a paper was published by Carl Frey and Michael Osborne, *How Susceptible are Jobs to Computerization?* They asserted that 47%

of U.S. employment was at risk of replacement by automation.[148] Their paper has been cited literally thousands of times. The authors examined a sample of 702 occupations by looking at the specific parts of the jobs that were susceptible to automation. They then generalized and concluded that most workers in transportation and logistics, in production and in office and administrative support were at risk. They also found that a large portion of service occupations were susceptible to computerization. Their analysis demonstrated that low-skill, low-wage jobs will be replaced in the near future. They assert that it is only those who develop creative and social skills who will find work in the future. Their analysis, therefore, has powerful implications for education, from preschool through training programs and higher education.

Two economists who have written extensively on the future of work are Erik Brynjolfsson and Andrew McAfee. Their first book, The Race Against the Machine, was an analysis of the accelerating tech and the disappearance of jobs.[149] In their second book, The Second Machine Age they expanded on these themes discussing the displacement of human workers by digitization and artificial intelligence (AI).[150] They appear to agree with some of Frey's and Osborne's conclusions in the second book, although they seem to agree more with traditional economists doubting the joblessness will occur in the long-term. No one, however, can deny that jobs requiring minimal education are likely to disappear, and they do not. They strongly recommend upgrading education, an essential task for any future wage/salary work as low-skill jobs disappear. They also mention MOOCs, Massive Open Online Courses, in this context, something considered below under higher education. Another of their recommendations is to upgrade infrastructure, something that coincides with our recommendations concerning a Green New Deal, although they define infrastructure more broadly. They emphasize, as we have, the essential role of government in this process.[151]

---

148 Carl Benedikt Frey & Michael Osborne. (2013). *How Susceptible are Jobs to Computerization?* Oxford University Engineering Sciences Department and the Oxford Martin Programme on the Impacts of Future Technology. Available at: https://www.oxfordmartin.ox.ac.uk/downloads/academic/The_Future_of_Employment.pdf

149 Eric Brynjolfsson & Andrew McAfee. (2012). *Race Against the Machine: How the Digital Revolution is Accelerating Innovation, Driving Productivity, and Irreversibly Transforming Employment and the Economy.* Lexington, MA: Digital Frontiers Press.

150 Eric Brynjolfsson & Andrew McAfee. (2014). *The Second Machine Age: Work, Progress, and Prosperity in a Time of Brilliant Technologies.* New York: W.W. Norton.

151 Eric Brynjolfsson & Andrew McAfee. (2014). Op. cit. pp. 206ff.

If we are able to address the threats posed by climate change and take advantage of the opportunities presented by transition from fossil fuels, there is still the question of whether enough work will be available in the future to permit anything like full employment. This is also addressed in great detail by some of the other writers we have already cited, such as Ford, Bregman, Yang and Lowry.[152] Like the previously mentioned analysts, each of these writers shows how the kinds of jobs being supplanted by digitization, AI and robotics are not simply blue collar labor requiring minimal education and training but many white collar jobs as well. This is the reason that these authors support establishing a Universal Basic Income (UBI), which I also advocate in the next chapter.

From a market perspective, robotics, artificial intelligence and more generally the digitization of work are *disruptive technologies* or disruptive innovations. I mentioned this in reference to the replacement of fossil fuel by green tech citing Jeremy Rifkin and Kingsmill Bond. According to the Christensen Institute (CI), which searches out and analyzes such changes, disruptive tech "describes a process by which a product or service initially takes root in simple applications at the bottom of a market—typically by being less expensive and more accessible—and then relentlessly moves upmarket, eventually displacing established competitors."[153] What we are talking about here are disruptive technologies that are displacing individuals from traditional jobs.

More recently, numerous books have been written suggesting that the introduction of artificial intelligence (AI) represents a change that will lead to the eventual disappearance, not only of blue-collar jobs requiring little education, but white-collar jobs as well. This is predicted based on the rise and increasing sophistication of so-called large language models (LLMs). You are already familiar, I am sure, with many of these like ChatGPT and others. LLMs may replace many jobs that were once the exclusive domains of trained professionals, some extensively educated. Professions that are the most vulnerable include

---

152   Martin Ford. (2015). *The Rise of the Robots*. New York: Basic Books. Rutger Bregman. (2017). *Utopia for Realists: How We Can Build the Ideal World*. New York: Little, Brown and Company; Andrew Yang. (2018). *The War on Normal People*. New York: Hachette Books; Annie Lowrey. (2018). *Give People Money: How a Universal Basic Income Would End Poverty, Revolutionize Work, and Remake the World*. New York: Random House.

153   https://www.christenseninstitute.org/disruptive-innovations/

communicators in banking, insurance, energy production, media and communications, retail sales, and many others who rely heavily on the use of language. Some practices in health care may be partially addressed by LLMs. A recent account with an easy-to-understand list of the types of work that will be replaced is the first chapter in *Free Money* by Liberty Knox.[154]

The prime example of job replacement that has been going on for many years is manufacturing. Martin Ford describes this in his book.[155] Here is what has happened. There were 19.6 million manufacturing jobs in 1979. By 2000 the number had declined to about 17.5 million but at that point began falling precipitously to less than 12 million at the end of the Great Recession. By 2026 it has risen very slightly to 12.6 million.[156] Globalization, offshoring of jobs and the vicissitudes of trade account for part of this change, as companies have moved manufacturing operations outside the U.S., but automation of manufacturing has been a more important cause in recent years.

As robots and AI are adopted, more output can be produced with fewer and fewer workers. More products are being produced and more money is being made by corporate shareholders while utilizing a smaller workforce.

The Optimists

Some analysts are convinced that we are moving to a very different society and economic system in which many of the essentials that now require money will become nearly free to everyone. Their ideas are enticing to anyone who cares about the future of humanity and human happiness.

A widely read author and educator is Peter Diamandis. One of his books written with Steven Kotler is *Abundance: The Future is Better than You Think*.[157] They outline many changes that are already occurring that will make currently scarce items abundant. For example,

---

154 Liberty Knox. (2026). *AI and Work: How Artificial Intelligence is Reshaping Jobs, Income and the Future of Employment. This is Book 2: Free Money with SSI and UBI for All.* Liberty Knox. ISBN 9798283065823.
155 Op. cit. Martin Ford. *The Rise of the Robots*, pages 53-5.
156 Available at: https://www.macrotrends.net/3109/us-manufacturing-employment
157 Peter H. Diamandis & Steven Kotler. (2012). *Abundance: The Future is Better than You Think.* New York: Free Press.

arable land is destined to disappear and even under the best scenarios will be unable to feed the earth's burgeoning population, which might increase by 2 or 3 billion people by 2050. One part of a solution to this problem is to turn to vertical farming in which crops are raised in dense, highly controlled enclosed greenhouses that are arranged as floors in tall buildings. This idea was introduced earlier[158] and has been implemented.[159] If you are interested in Diamandis look at the online school, Singularity University, where courses are offered in understanding and adapting to the efficiencies brought on by technological innovation.[160]

Here I briefly contrast the views of two authors, mentioned above, Andrew McAfee and Jeremy Rifkin. McAfee's book, *More from Less,* is a startling account of the benefits of technological change, at least to those of us who attended graduate school during the age of dire predictions about running out of resources.[161] He documents how economic growth has continued in the US (and elsewhere) while at the same time the use of resources has begun to decline. These include all the categories of resources that were predicted to run out in the present century, such as metals of nearly all kinds, wood and paper, fertilizer, water for crops, and others, including plastics. More is being produced while using significantly fewer resources. The driver of this process, McAfee asserts, is competition in capitalist society leading to technological innovation. He is a staunch defender of capitalism within social democracies and sees this process as continuing so long as competition (as opposed to monopolies) continues as a driver of corporate innovation. But McAfee is not a climate-change denier. Indeed, he sees the possibilities for the remainder of the 21st Century as somewhere between bad and catastrophically bad. He notes in multiple passages the importance of laws and tax policies in controlling negative externalities of corporations—in this case the effects of greenhouse gas pollution.

---

158   Dickson Despommier. (2010). *The Vertical Farm: Feeding the World in the 21ˢᵗ Century.* New York: St. Martin's Press.

159   For example, see: https://roboticsandautomationnews.com/2019/05/03/top-25-vertical-farming-companies/22181/

160   https://su.org/

161   Andrew McAfee. (2019). More from Less: The Surprising Story of How We Learned to Prosper Using Fewer Resources—and What Happens Next. New York: Scribner

Competition then is promoted as the driving force of tech innovation and coming abundance. In that light, an interesting question may come to mind as you read McAfee's book. Can capitalist corporations, as we now know them, survive this process. For example, he emphasizes the importance of 3D printing in increasing manufacturing efficiency. There is a problem with this. I have worked with 3D printing for several years. There are innovations literally every week in the materials utilized, printing speeds, and large-scale printing. 3D design programs have become easier and easier to learn and use. It is now possible for individuals and small communities to produce a variety of items for everyday needs on demand in their own homes or neighborhoods. Imagine that you need a new shirt or blouse. Rather than going to a store or an online retailer, you recycle your old garment and use your 3D printer to print out a new one using freely available shared models available online. What happens to corporations that produce clothes when that happens? Some might say, okay but the printers themselves have to be manufactured. No, because as any current user will tell you many of the non-metallic parts in the printers are themselves printed. Metal parts can now be printed. For example, I recently printed some metal sculptures using metal-in-plastic materials that I then completed in a cheap metal oven. Granted you say, but surely big things could not be produced. No, houses and cars and boats are already being printed. One can imagine future coops that own machines of this type and use them to meet virtually all the material needs of their members. What happens to manufacturers of such items in that context?

That brings us to an earlier book by Jeremy Rifkin in which he outlined ideas relevant to the survival of capitalism. The book is *The Zero Marginal Cost Society: The Internet of Things, the Collaborative Commons, and the Eclipse of Capitalism.*[162] Rifkin identifies a number of areas in which productive efficiency has increased to the point that the cost to produce one more unit is essentially free, after fixed costs have been recovered. A good example is eBook and online music publishing. Marginal cost refers to the cost of producing one more unit of a product, such as one more kilowatt-hour of electricity after the capital costs of the power plant have been recovered or one more

162 Jeremy Rifkin. (2014). *The Zero Marginal Cost Society: The Internet of Things, the Collaborative Commons, and the Eclipse of Capitalism.* New York: Palgrave McMillan Trade.

eBook after the capital costs of the production hardware and software have been recouped. This is what I was referring to in the discussion of future free energy from solar and wind. Rifkin sees a possible society in which various "commons" replace private corporations and the goods necessary to live a normal life can be produced practically for free. Because I have already referenced Rifkin's later book on the Green New Deal, you will not be surprised that he also addresses the possible serious consequences of global warming in this earlier book. Indeed, in one of his final chapters he describes in graphic detail what he calls the "climate change wildcard." Whether it should be called a wildcard is debatable since it is certain to happen if we continue on the current path.

Finally, a short and clearly written but less well-known book by Matt Greer, is Our Future is Free.[163] His is a utopian vision that we can hope comes to pass. In Greer's future world, work is replaced by automation, competition is replaced by cooperation, scarcity is replaced by abundance, ownership is replaced by access, the monetary system is replaced by a resource-based system. In that future world there is no money, and because all families have access to resources, children no longer need money.

In the short-term we cannot count on any of these visions coming to fruition unless we face up to the virtual certainty of unaddressed climate changes. So, any solutions to the problems of economic hardship of families with children must first be planned within the short-term context but allow for longer-term changes. That is the reason I advocate a slow but steady adoption of Universal Basic Income (UBI) in the following chapter.

---

163 Matt Greer. (2017). Our Future is Free. Independently Published. Available at: https://books.google.
com/books/about/Our_Future_Is_Free.html?id=k6iPswEACAAJ

Chapter 8

Solutions

This chapter is a further consideration of solutions that might improve the financial situation of a significant proportion of American families.

Government programs that are *targeted,* even those in combination with private enterprise, tend to be less acceptable to the general public. Solutions based on characteristics of families, like the amount of earned income, family structure, gender, locality, and so on should be avoided if possible. Medicaid, TANF (cash welfare), SNAP (food stamps), School Lunches and WIC (Special Supplemental Nutrition Program for Women, Infants and Children) are examples of targeted solutions. Targeted programs for poor and working-class individuals and families are often regarded negatively, as foolish and wasteful giveaways to lazy takers. Replacing targeted programs with *universal* programs eliminates the basis of those arguments.

Universal means programs offered to all individuals or families without regard to their income levels or other characteristics. Examples of universal benefits in the US, at least among the elderly, are Social Security and Medicare. These are government welfare programs that are strongly supported across the entire U.S. population. Look at the reaction to attempts to privatize social security or recall the old folks protesting the Affordable Care Act but walking around with signs saying, "Hands Off My Medicare!"

Universality assumes some level of acceptance of everyone else in society, a sense of *community.* The problem is that American society is becoming more diverse and diversity can breed misunderstanding and mistrust. As a side effect, universal programs can foster a sense of community, of everyone being in this together. Another positive change is that the millennial generation, particularly those born after the turn of the century, are more accepting of diversity than their parents and grandparents were.[164] One of the most effective means of overcoming the lack of understanding and trust of others who are different from us is interaction. Working together on common projects, for example, can foster understanding and trust. Interaction and ongoing relationships are also powerful counters to stereotypes. And, apart from issues of respect and social justice, diversity has many positive social and economic benefits.

Solutions are described with some pros and cons in three areas: direct services programs, public service and private employment, and Universal Basic Income (UBI). These sections are followed by proposals for how they might be combined with the changing contexts already considered. Then we look at how solutions might be financed.

Solution 1: Direct Service Programs

In this section the traditional approach to improving the lot of families is considered: government support and service programs. One of these—universal health care—should be enacted immediately simply to bring the U.S. into line with every other developed nation in the world. Furthermore, relief of the burdens of massive student loan debt that so many young American now endure must be directly addressed. Universal preschool and universal higher education should also be considered. All the other programs discussed are targeted at the present time. It would be best to find ways of replacing them with universal approaches.

Universal Health Care

Access to health care has come to be regarded as a basic human right in every other developed nation on earth and in many poorer countries. The United States lags far behind all other advanced societies in this regard. In Chapter 1, the skyrocketing costs of health care under the for-profit system in the United States was described. It is at

---

164   See Paul Taylor. *The Next America*, cited earlier. For example, page 75.

least twice as expensive as in other nations, yet health care outcomes are poorer. Millions are effectively denied health care because of the expense, and those who become ill and must seek care, but do not possess the financial resources to pay for it, experience years of crippling debt. Most Americans recognize the need for universal health care.

Universal in this case means that health care is provided to all citizens.[165] How universal health care is organized varies from country to country, but all involve strict government regulation. In some, such as Canada, it is a government program similar to the U.S. Medicare system but available to everyone regardless of age. In these, the government controls prices and fees paid to providers and the cost of drugs and medications. In some other countries, care is provided through insurance, although unlike the U.S., the insurance system is nonprofit. In countries utilizing this kind of system, such as Germany, Switzerland and Japan, the government controls costs through regulation. There are also combinations of these two approaches in which providers are private, but the insurance system is government operated. A clear and detailed discussion can be found PNHP (Physicians for a National Health Program) website.[166]

Americans seem to be largely unaware of how far the US had lagged behind other countries in health care. Here is a list of countries that offer universal health care to their citizens. This list is from Wikipedia showing variations by county.[167] Granted that it is offered in different ways and there are variations in the quality of the care provided. But the US has millions who have no access to health care at all, unless they can personally pay and, as we have noted, US health care is the most expensive in the world by far but with poorer outcomes. If you are an American, peruse this list and be embarrassed:

Africa

Algeria, Botswana, Burkina Faso, Mauritius, Rwanda, Seychelles, Tunisia

---

165   The International Insurance website has a brief discussion and list of countries with universal programs. Available at: https://www.internationalinsurance.com/health/countries-free-healthcare.php

166   Available at: http://www.pnhp.org/single_payer_resources/health_care_systems_four_basic_models.php Click on the Latest News links to see what is going on currently.

167   Source is Wikipedia at: https://en.wikipedia.org/wiki/List_of_countries_with_universal_health_care. The article offers summaries of the methods and restrictions of the system in each country.

Asia

Azerbaijan, Bhutan, China, Cyprus, Hong Kong, India, Indonesia, Israel, Japan, Kuwait, Macau, Malaysia, Maldives, Pakistan, Philippines, Saudi Arabia, Singapore, South Korea, North Korea, Sri Lanka, Taiwan, Thailand, Turkey, United Arab Emirates

Europe

Albania, Armenia, Austria, Belgium, Croatia, Czech Republic, Denmark, Estonia, Finland, France, Georgia, Germany, Greece, Iceland, Ireland, Italy, Latvia, Lithuania, Luxembourg, Netherlands, Norway, North Macedonia, Poland, Portugal, Romania, Russia, Serbia, Spain, Sweden, Switzerland, United Kingdom, England, Northern Ireland, Scotland, Wales, Isle of Man

North America

Bahamas, Canada, Costa Rica, Cuba, Mexico, Trinidad and Tobago,

South America

Argentina, Brazil, Chile, Colombia, Suriname, Oceania, Australia, New Zealand

Universal Higher Education

A point often made by pundits and policy analysts is that, whatever education's value in enhancing minds and lives, a better education usually translates into a better lifetime income. Income levels are strongly correlated with level of education. For example, in 2024 the median annual income for a householder with no high school diploma was $36,900. For one with a diploma or GED but no college, it was $58,410. Some college raised it to $76,520. Those with a bachelor's degree or higher averaged $132,700. These are U.S. Census figures.[168] Analysts argue that better education would alleviate many of the financial problems experienced by those in the lower income portion of the population.

---

168 Available at: https://www.census.gov/library/stories/2025/09/education-and-income.html

Higher education is associated with better paying jobs and the kinds of jobs available for people with more limited education have declined. But how many individuals in the U.S. can afford to get a four-year college degree? A college education in the United States is expensive. For four-year institutions, the average yearly tuition, fees, books, room and board, and other expenses during the period from 2012 to 2023 was around $10,000 for public institutions, $40,000 for private nonprofit schools and in the range of $19,000 for private for-profits. The exact yearly figures can be found in a publication from the National Center for Education Statistics (NCES).[169] This means that the average cost for a four year degree would be around $40,000 in a public institution but considerably more in private schools. For most individuals and families, student loans are the only solution. In 2025 total student loan debt in the U.S. was around $1.8 trillion, the largest part of U.S. debt, outside of mortgages. This problem should be addressed. Relief of student debt, even at this level, is clearly doable in an economy that generated at GDP of over $31 trillion in 2025.

A better approach would be to make higher education, like grade school and high school, freely available to everyone. To some this will seem to be yet another example of mindless giveaways, but even a cursory look at other countries reveals that free higher education is common.

While there is no national program in the United States, some states are covering tuition and fees at public community institutions: West Virginia, Nevada, Arkansas, Michigan, Rhode Island, Maine, Massachusetts, Kentucky, California, and Louisiana. The length and extent of coverage vary. Detailed info is available in a summary by Chris Kissell.[170] Here is a list of countries that provide free college education to their citizens:

Cuba, Mexico, Egypt, Philippines, Morocco, Sri Lanka, New Zealand, Uruguay, Trinidad and Tobago, Mauritius, Fiji, India, Turkey, Argentina, Poland, Taiwan, Lebanon, Estonia, Luxembourg, Russia, Brazil, Czechia, Iran, Cyprus, Germany, Kenya, Saudi Arabia, United Arab Emirates, Norway, Slovakia, Kuwait, Panama, Lithuania, Brunei,

---

169   Available at: https://nces.ed.gov/fastfacts/display.asp?id=76
170   Available at: https://www.moneytalksnews.com/slideshows/states-that-offer-free-tuition-to-residents/

Iceland, France, Italy, Spain, Belgium, Sweden, Greece, Austria, Denmark, Slovenia, Malta, Finland.[171]

For education to be even a partial solution to the economic hardship of families, the cost and debt issues will have to be addressed. Higher education could be a partial solution for American families and their children but only if it is made free for all who qualify. The U.S. needs to catch up. The programs in selected states may indicate that we are moving in that direction.

A much lower cost alternative are massive open online courses (MOOCS) as referenced earlier. For example, Coursera offers hundreds of undergraduate and graduate courses and several graduate-level degrees. Many courses are free but fees are generally required for grading of assignments and obtaining certificates. However, compared to tuition costs just mentioned, the fees are modest: $59 per month.[172] In the absence of federal government support for free universal higher education, this type of education and training may be at least a part of the future of higher education in the United States.

Universal Preschool and Pre-K Education

Early childhood education (ECE) refers to teaching of children up to the age of eight years, that is through the third grade. Kindergarten is a subset of ECE designating programs for children prior to entering first grade.

Pre-Kindergarten (Pre-K) is a more restricted category referring to educational programs for children beginning before their fifth birthday that children usually enter at age 4. Preschool education typically refers to education of children in 2-4 years age range. Thus, preschool and pre-K definitions seem to overlap somewhat. I will use the term preschool encompassing both.

Jhalak Sharma has recently written a summary of the key benefits of early childhood education.[173] Some earlier work demonstrates the benefits clearly. Formal preschool education for children has beneficial long-term outcomes for the children themselves as they grow into

---

171   Available at: https://worldpopulationreview.com/country-rankings/countries-with-free-college

172   Available at: https://www.coursera.org/courseraplus/

173   Available at: https://www.21kschool.com/us/blog/benefits-of-early-childhood-education/

adulthood and for society generally. A good set of summary papers can be found on the Heckman website that show human benefits. For example, the Carolina Abecedarian Project (ABC) and the Carolina Approach to Responsive Education (CARE) programs were evaluated in field experiments similar to the studies described in earlier chapters. They provided nutrition, health care and early education for experimental children aged 0 to 5 years. Follow-ups on these children later in life show comparative positive effects on education and employment, such as rates of high school graduation, number of years of education, increased incomes, lower drug use. In addition, there were a variety of long-term health benefits.[174] The Heckman studies examined the economic benefits to society showing that the costs of universal 0 to 5 years preschool programs were more than offset by the benefits to society as a whole. A recent study by Elizabeth Cascio, *Does Universal Preschool Hit the Target? Program Access and Preschool Impacts,* also demonstrates the educational value and how financial benefits to society outweigh the costs.[175] Another paper by Arthur Rolnick, *Investing in Early Childhood Development is Smart Economic Development,* shows the economic benefits of government investment in high quality early childhood education. For every $1 invested there is a $4 to $16 return through increased worker productivity, lower education costs, reduced crime and less government assistance.[176]

Universal preschool would be just that—untargeted and available to all. As discussed earlier, money affects the performance of children in school. Universal preschool does not provide additional money to families but addresses directly educational needs of children.

Concerning programs in the U.S. educating four-year olds, only four states (Florida, Oklahoma, Vermont and Wisconsin) and the District of Columbia in 2024 funded universal pre-k for two-thirds or more of their 4-year-old children. Eight other states had enrollments

---

174 Read the summary of these studies at: https://heckmanequation.org/www/assets/2017/01/F_Heckman_CBAOnePager_120516.pdf . Many other papers and presentations are available on the website: https://heckmanequation.org/top-20-resources/

175 Elizabeth U. Cascio. (2019). *Does Universal Preschool Hit the Target?* Program Access and Preschool Impacts. Dartmouth College. Available at: https://www.nber.org/papers/w23215

176 Arthur Rolnick. (2015). *Investing in Early Childhood Development is Smart Economic Development.* Wisconsin Family Impact Seminars. Available at: https://www.purdue.edu/hhs/hdfs/fii/wp-content/uploads/2015/07/s_wifis32c01.pdf

at lower levels but generally above 50% (Alabama, California, Georgia, Iowa, New Mexico, New York, West Virginia, and Wisconsin).[177]

Universal or very high enrollment preschool is available nationwide in numerous other countries for children in the 3-5 year age range. Here is a list of the top ten with percentage enrollments in the 96-99% range for children of this age: France, Belgium, Spain, Italy, United Kingdom, Demark, Norway, Sweden, South Korea, and Iceland.

The U.S. needs to catch up.

Guaranteed Housing

Moving on to targeted programs, the problems of massive homelessness and the shortage of affordable rental housing in the United States were presented in earlier chapter along considerations of the effects of unsafe and unhealthy housing. There is great interest in housing at the local level, particularly in large urban areas, but interestingly very little discussion seems to occur at the national level.

The United States fares poorly when compared to other developed countries in universal health care, universal higher education and universal preschool. This is also true for housing. A recent study by Michael Carliner and Ellen Marya, *Rental Housing, An International Comparison*, illustrates this. They compare 12 countries in Europe and North American. Looking at the cost burden of renting, compared to Canada and European countries, the U.S. had the greatest percentage (50.6%) of renters who spend more than 30% of their pre-tax household income on rent. Some countries were nearly as high: Belgium (46.9%) and the UK (48.0%). But several others were substantially less; for example: Italy (26.9%), Austria (19.8%) and Switzerland (18.2%). And, the U.S. had the greatest share of renters who spend over half their income on rent (27.8%). This statistic was lower in all other countries ranging from 3.6% in Switzerland to 20.3% in the UK. According to this study, the differences are due in part to income inequality, which is greater in the U.S. than in Canada and Europe. It is also the result of the type of available housing. For example, in the U.S. more rental units are higher-priced single-family detached homes. Finally,

---

177 A short summary is available at: https://www.ecs.org/wp-content/uploads/Universal-Pre-K-Landscape_2025.pdf. It considers two studies in 2024 of preschool education from the National Institute for Early Education Research, available at: https://nieer.org/yearbook/2024

housing vouchers in the U.S. are not an "entitlement" that must be provided to every family meeting the eligibility requirements. Only a minority of American households that meet the requirements actually receive a voucher. In other countries there are no such limits—eligible households receive the benefit. The authors qualify these differences in various ways noting the difficulty of cross-national comparisons where benefit levels, types of housing, quality standards and other factors come into play. However, the basic thrust of the analysis is that the richest country—the United States—fares worst in the comparisons.[178]

As noted in Chapter 1, 771,480 individuals were homeless in the U.S. on any single day in 2024. A substantial minority of these are children. Costly programs exist to deal with the effects of homelessness. I was reflecting on how often my colleagues and I encountered homelessness in our evaluation studies of widely varying programs. For example, homeless families and families recently evicted or on the verge of being evicted make up a substantial subset of the cases reported for child neglect. We saw hundreds of such families in our studies. Here is a monograph I presented at the 2014 National Conference on Ending Family and Youth Homelessness that summarizes findings of some of the research described in Chapter 2.[179] Another example: the majority of cases in an evaluation we conducted of an urban mental health/drug court diversion program were homeless individuals arrested for vagrancy and related offenses.[180] A third example: we did a study of a program that used busing to keep children in homeless families in the same school rather than shifting schools as their families had to move. In each of these substantial money and professional effort was expended dealing with the effects of eviction and homelessness.

The most obvious solution to homelessness and housing problems is to provide housing vouchers based on income. In his book *Evicted*, Matthew Desmond advocates an expansion of the current U.S. voucher program to all low-income families. The program would be means-

---

178 Michael Carliner & Ellen Marya. (2016). *Rental Housing: An International Comparison*. Working paper from the Joint Center for Housing Studies of Harvard University. Available at: https://www.jchs.harvard.edu/sites/default/files/international_rental_housing_carliner_marya.pdf

179 L. Anthony Loman. (2014). *Flexible Assistance to Families Encountered by the Child Welfare System: Focus on Housing and Housing-Related Help*. Institute of Applied Research. Available at: http://www.iarstl.org/papers/FlexibleAssistance&Housing.pdf

180 Michael M. Orehuela & L. Anthony Loman. (2010). *City of St. Louis Jail Diversion Project. Institute of Applied Research*. Available at: http://www.iarstl.org/papers/StLouisJailDiversionReport.pdf

tested, that is, it would be a targeted one in which families below a certain income level would be eligible for a housing voucher. The voucher could be used anywhere for any type of housing the family desired. He suggests that families might be required to utilize 30% of their income for housing with the voucher covering any additional cost.[181] The law establishing the program would need to require landlords to honor vouchers and protect against discrimination. It would also doubtless require rent-control laws to prevent gouging, perhaps similar to the strict laws in place in New York City. Rent control would need to be tailored to each region and locale because of widely varying costs of housing.

Food Programs

In Chapter 1, food insecurity was examined with many examples from my research. This occurs in spite of the existence the Supplemental Nutrition Assistance Program or SNAP—food stamps. The uselessness of the work requirements that have been tacked onto this program were demonstrated in that chapter. The problem is not that SNAP recipients do not work or that they are more averse to work than other people. The majority of those who can work *have jobs while they are on food stamps*! It is rather that their pay is deficient. If you want to learn more, read Dottie Rosenbaum's paper on SNAP and work.[182] In the short term, SNAP must be continued and expanded. However, work requirements and other invidious practices, like drug testing of applicants, should be dropped.

Cash to Families with Children

I described what has happened under the Targeted Assistance for Needy Families (TANF) program after it replaced the earlier Aid to Families with Dependent Children (AFDC) in the mid-1990s. As shown earlier, experimental studies focused on expanding Employment and Training (E&T) requirements did not produce positive outcomes. Rather positive outcomes occur when cash to families is increased. The

---

181 Matthew Desmond. (2016). *Evicted: Poverty and Profit in the American City.* New York: Crown Publishers. See pages 308-313.

182 A good paper in this regard is: Dottie Rosenbaum. (2013). *The Relationship Between SNAP and Work Among Low-Income Households.* Center for Budget and Policy Priorities. Available at: https://www.cbpp.org/sites/default/files/atoms/files/1-29-13fa.pdf

useless work requirements in TANF should be dropped. And in the process, legislators should reintroduce the word CHILDREN back into its name, perhaps, the Benefits to Families with Children Program (BFCP).

But a better solution would be to make the program universal, at least for families with children, similar to the German Child Benefit program (Kindergeld) mentioned above. The German program is available to all families with children and in 2025 amounted to between 255 Euros ($296) per month for each child. It continues until the child reaches age 18 but may be extended to age 25 for children who pursue further education. There are special provisions for children with disabilities of various kinds permitting the payments to extend beyond even this age. The beautiful thing about this approach is that it eliminates the routine maker-taker stereotyping and political grousing about giveaways and handouts associated with cash welfare programs. More importantly, it is an immense benefit to children.

A broader and untargeted solution that could produce the same results is a Universal Basic Income. A UBI would provide a benefit payment to each adult, like the North Caroline Cherokee program or the Mincome program discussed in Chapter 5. The UBI solution is discussed further below.

There are a number of valuable targeted programs, like WIC and School Lunches, that could be discussed, but I stop with the ones just described. If government service programs should be part of the solution, these are some of the options. If the universal programs in health care, higher education and preschool were enacted nationally the United States would become comparable to other countries. I can already hear the moans and cries that the "costs would be astronomical." So, diligent deliberation should occur before enacting them, like the hour or so of deep consideration that occurred before the vote on rent-seeking trillion+ dollar giveaway enshrined in the 2017 federal tax cuts.

Solution 2: Public Service Employment and Public-Private Employment

Some analysts reject UBI as a solution, instead suggesting a FJG (Federal Jobs Guarantee). FJG is primarily a large-scale version of an approach that made up part of the employment and training efforts beginning in the 1970s, namely Public Service Employment (PSE), except in this case, the program seeks to insure that everyone who wants to work has a job. My colleagues and I were very familiar with PSE because some of our early program evaluation projects were of state and local employment and training (E&T) efforts that offered PSE as part of their E&T package.

The term *full employment* always arises when a job guarantee is discussed. A Federal Jobs Guarantee assumes that anyone who wants to work will be assisted. If they cannot find a private sector job the government will provide a job. Advocates assume that a wage from a job (as opposed to free money) is the solution or a major part of the solution to avoiding economic hardship and living a fulfilled and happy life.

To be effective a Federal Jobs Guarantee would have to do two things. First it would have to ensure jobs for everyone so that full employment might be achieved. Secondly, it would also have to ensure that the pay received was sufficient to provide a living wage. Recall the discussion of minimum wage, poverty level wages and living wages.

A recent and clearly argued proposal for an FJG by Randal Wray and associates uses a more traditional terminology: *Public Service Employment: A Path to Full Employment.*[183] This paper lays out the types of jobs that might be funded. Readers can find them by going to the online PDF. They include scores of possible jobs in three areas: care for the environment, care for the community and care for people. Particularly in the last area, the jobs listed include many that would not be considered to be "work" in the traditional sense but rather "women's work," as we discuss below in reference to a Universal Basic Income.

Some of the negative criticisms of a Federal Jobs Guarantee are that it would increase the size of government, that it would be inflationary, that it would drive private employers out of business, that because of its size it would be difficult to administer, and that most of the jobs would be useless make-work.

---

183 L. Randall Wray, Flavia Dantas, Scott Fullwiler, Pavlina R. Tcherneva & Stephanie A. Kelton. (2018). *Public Service Employment: A Path to Full Employment.* Levy Economics Institute of Bard College. Available at: http://www.levyinstitute.org/pubs/rpr_4_18.pdf

The first of these is obvious and leads to consideration of possible combined public-private solutions. The second is possible, if the program is purely governmental and requires that living wages be paid, although those making proposals of this kind argue that this problem can be handled. The third is both true and laughable at the same time—as if the US government has no experience in handling millions of workers (such as soldiers and military civilians). However, the immense expense of administering another targeted program involving millions of jobs would be enormous. The fourth does not have to be true as a perusal of the suggested jobs in the paper by Randal Wray and associates shows.[184]

The debate about a jobs guarantee hinges in part on whether full employment is the only solution to the current problem of unemployment and underemployment. People on both sides of the argument seem to assume that the only way that individuals and families can be economically secure (and also happy, fulfilled and free from vices) is through ***work***. As discussed in the next section, we can ask whether paid employment in traditional jobs will be the life-solution for all citizens in the long term.

Solution 3: Universal Basic Income (UBI)

Universal Basic Income (UBI) was considered earlier. UBI is based on a relatively simple idea. Every adult in a given society receives an equal amount of money periodically. UBI is not means-tested or targeted nor is it tied to work.

The concept has a growing entourage of policy and social activists as well as policymakers themselves around the world. I mentioned BIEN (Basic Income Earth Network) earlier. Bien is a longstanding organization that began in Europe several decades ago and now has thousands of members worldwide. Papers and news reports are listed daily on its website (https://basicincome.org/). The books on UBI mentioned so far are a small fraction of many books currently being published on the subject. Nonetheless, a debate is ongoing between supporters of the approach and those who are opposed to it. For

---

184 Op. cit. Wray et al. *Public Service Employment.* Available at: http://www.levyinstitute.org/pubs/rpr_4_18.pdf

more recent books, I would suggest Universal Basic Income by Karl Widerquist or Basic Income: *The Policy that Changes Everything* by Matthew Johnson and Associates.[185]

Arguments for Universal Basic Income. A basic argument for a UBI is that it would be just that—universal. It would avoid the stigma associated with targeted welfare programs in which some, perhaps many, who do not qualify for the program become resentful of others receiving something for free that they do not. The Alaska Permanent Fund where each adult received $2,000 a year—at least before the state legislature began reducing it—is a good example. No citizen there resents the payment because *every adult* receives it.

Another argument supporting a UBI in line with this book is that it would alleviate and ultimately eliminate the current economic hardship experienced by millions of American families. This would depend on the level of the payments. Looking back on the consideration of *living wages*, we can ask how large would such payments have to be to accomplish this feat. I use the 2025 data presented in the first chapter to illustrate how UBI might increase family income. Dependent on when you are reading this, the amounts will have to be updated to account for inflation.

A $1,000/month payment to adults would come close to accomplishing accomplish this in many two-adult families who were also working minimum wage jobs at current levels. Looking at the Claiborne Parish example of living wage from Chapter 1, $7.25/hour for two adults working fulltime comes to $30,160 per year, assuming 2080 hours of yearly work. Adding $24,000 from a $1,000/month UBI to two adults would raise the total income to $54,160 or an equivalent wage of $26.03/hour. This approaches the level of a living wage in this locale of $28.48 for families with 2 children and 2 working adults. However, a more modest approach in which payments start out lower and increase progressively over several years may have a better chance of succeeding. Guy Standing, cited previously, is one of the leading lights advocating a UBI. Standing indicates that perhaps baby steps are needed in starting out. He suggests a more measured approach in

---

185 Karl Widerquist. (2024). *Universal Basic Income.* Cambridge, MA: The MIT Press. Matthew Johnson, Kate Pickett, Daniel Nettle, Howard Reed, Elliot Johnson & Ian Robson, (2025). *Basic Income: The Policy that Changes Everything.* Bristol, UK: Bristol University Press.

which a small UBI is introduced and increases over time while targeted programs are reduced.[186]

Another advantage is that a basic income payment would avoid the administrative cost associated with various targeted programs. It would be as simple to administer as current payments in the Social Security system.

It would also provide a new level of republican freedom, as Standing indicates.[187] For example, it would make it possible for individuals to turn down an onerous or boring job. This would mean that employers would have to offer better pay for such jobs. It would make it possible for individuals to engage in creative work that might not be compensated for in the current economic system. Other examples are: the freedom to have a child, the freedom to become educated or trained, the freedom to start a business venture, the freedom to stay in a low-paying job. These are some of the ethical arguments made in support of UBI. Readers will find other advantages argued in the referenced books.

There are many objections to UBI. Guy Standing, quoting from Albert Hirschmann's *Rhetoric of Reaction*, points out three types of attacks to big new social policy ideas: 1) futility (it cannot work), 2) perversity (there would be negative consequences), and 3) jeopardy (it would endanger other goals).[188] He points out that such objections were raised to the introduction of unemployment benefits, family benefits and social security in the US but faded away after the programs were introduced and accepted.

The first objection is that it would cost too much. This is a jeopardy argument. We have already considered the costs of rent seeking. Take the low capital gains tax rates utilized mainly by those in the upper 1% of incomes. If the rates were comparable to individual income tax rates on high incomes and someone suggested lowering them to 20%, there might be an outcry that it would cost too much! But since the rate is already low and has been low for many years, this form of welfare

---

186 Guy Standing. (2017). *Basic Income: A Guide for the Open-Minded.* New Haven: Yale University Press, pages 293-5.

187 Ibid. Chapter 3, pages 47-70.

188 Op. cit. Standing, Basic Income, p. 111, citing: Albert Hirschman. (1991). *The Rhetoric of Reaction: Perversity, Futility, Jeopardy.* Cambridge, MA: Harvard University Press

seems to fit into one of the many blind spots of critics who decry giveaways. One approach might be to place a modest fee on all forms of rentierism. Another much discussed solution to the cost objection is to reduce or eliminate current targeted programs each of which involves large bureaucracies of workers whose jobs, among others, are to qualify applicants, to monitor participants to avoid cheating and to make sure they engage in employment and training programs. What would a UBI cost?

Robert Greenstein argues that the cost for the US would be $3 trillion/year for a program that paid $10,000 a year to every adult.[189] Annie Lowrey, who supports a UBI, suggests $3.9 trillion/year for a program offering $1,000/month (thus, $12,000/year).[190] There are many other estimates, all in the $2 trillion plus range. For example, Andy Stern who is another supporter estimates $2.7 trillion/year for the same level of payments. Figures like these are sometimes, as in the case of Greenstein, meant to show that basic income proposals are simply pie-in-the-sky impossible. Greenstein makes the jeopardy argument as follows: you could not increase taxes to pay for basic income in the face of all the additional taxes that will have to be levied to address the solvency of Social Security and Medicare, our crumbling infrastructure and other pressing needs. The same kinds of objections are raised by those who are opposed to universal health care in the US, although they have a hard time explaining how every other developed nation in the world somehow pays for health care for all their citizens without going bankrupt. Other analysts of UBI, like Lowrey and Stern, are trying to be realistic while at the same time offering ways to finance basic income in the US. They are saying that there are difficulties but they can be dealt with.

A second objection is the threat to full employment. We mentioned that analysts advocating a Federal Jobs Guarantee (FJG) seem to believe that keeping people working is critical. By work is meant the kinds of paid labor that constitute jobs in the traditional workplace. For many across the political spectrum, work legitimizes the reception of

189 Robert Greenstein. (2019). Commentary: Universal Basic Income may Sound Attractive but, if it occurred, Would Likelier Increase Poverty Rather than Reducing it. Center on Budget and Policy Priorities. Available at: https://www.cbpp.org/poverty-and-opportunity/commentary-universal-basic-income-may-sound-attractive-but-if-it-occurred

190 Op. cit. Chapter 10, p. 184.v

money but also is a key to human happiness. Through jobs people find purpose, feelings of competence and mastery. Without work people become bored. Work is a way to avoid indolence and the vices that may result. For these reasons simply giving people money, they argue, will lead to unhappiness, inactivity and vice. For the working class, free money is seen as illegitimate, even immoral. These may seem extreme views but if you read some of the negative commentaries on UBI you will come away with the sense that the commentators share to some extent in these beliefs.

Of course, there are plenty of crummy jobs. Among these are the ones we discussed earlier that pay less than a poverty wage and only a fraction of a living wage. However, it is questionable whether paid work in general provides the fulfillment that is often assumed. For example, in a Conference Board national survey of employees conducted about one month before the present writing, 56% reported feeling overall satisfied with their jobs. That means that nearly half of respondents *were not satisfied* overall with their jobs. When we look at the components of work around 60% ± 6% were dissatisfied with their wages, health plan, family leave plan, workload and recognition or acknowledgement.[191] Majorities are less than satisfied with some things often assumed to be a natural outcome of having a job.

Certain blind spots are also apparent in the belief system about paid work. Free money from the government to ordinary working adults is viewed as illegitimate. However, other sources of money that do not involve work and are essentially free are not questioned. Inherited money is free but legitimate. Becoming rich because your parents or grandparents passed on money to you is okay. Returns on investments often involve little work but are still considered legitimate. Does it seem strange to you that risking one's capital is equated with virtuous work. The examples of welfare for large corporations and the rich considered above under changing context 3 often go unquestioned. Skimming of government funds or evading taxes under rentierism is seen as perfectly legitimate. Also, excluded from the definition of work are numerous unpaid activities. These include parenting, cooking and

---

191 The Conference Board. (2019). *Poll: Job Satisfaction Climbs to its Highest Levels in over Two Decades.* Available at: https://www.prnewswire.com/news-releases/poll-job-satisfaction-climbs-to-highest-level-in-over-two-decades-300909167.html

house cleaning for one's family, care of elderly or disabled relatives, volunteer community service activities. Much of this is what has traditionally been defined as women's work. No one denies that these activities are valuable and often tedious and tiring, but they do not seem to be included in the definition of work leading to a happy and fulfilled life.

Regarding work and basic income, two things can then be said. First, a basic income would not prohibit work and does not lead to abandonment of work. All the large-scale studies in both developed and developing countries of which I am aware support this conclusion. The exceptions to this rule are that mothers sometimes reduce their work in order to spend time with their children and youths in families receiving a UBI sometimes are found to work less. The studies we described in Chapter 3—the Cherokee project in North Carolina, the Mincome project in Canada and the US experiments, did not result in significant work reduction.

Secondly, basic income payments may be viewed as broadening the definition of work. Advocates assume that valuable human activities, such as giving birth to children, caring for and educating them, and many other types of so-called women's work that advance the general interests and welfare of society should be compensated. Basic income would not do away with these kinds of work. It would make it possible to engage in them without the economic hardship of joblessness or of jobs that do not pay a living wage. The book to read that explains this most clearly is the earlier cited reference: Annie Lowrey's book, *Give People Money: How Universal Basic Income would End Poverty, Revolutionize Work and Remake the World.*[192] In Chapter 8 she cites studies showing that women's unpaid care work around the world would amount to $12 trillion annually were it compensated at minimum wage levels. As she says "unpaid care workers provide the infrastructure that lets formal labor exist."[193] This implies another advantage that Lowrey stresses but has also been emphasized elsewhere. Basic income would validate the value of all human contributions to the ongoing functioning of society.

---

192 Annie Lowrey. (2018). *Give People Money: How a Universal Basic Income Would End Poverty, Revolutionize Work, and Remake the World.* New York: Random House

193 Ibid. p. 151.

Could the Proposed Programs be Created?

Are these anything other than pipe dreams? Would Americans support the kinds of changes we have suggested?

First, do Americans agree that climate change is a critical problem in need of action by the federal government? As of this writing, some decline has occurred regarding human-driven climate change from a high of around 60% in 2018. Yet, according to a 2025 poll by the University of Chicago, over half (53%) of Americans expressed a belief that climate change is mostly caused by humans. That climate change is happening and that the Federal government should warn citizens about weather is accepted by over three-quarters (76%) of Americans.[194]

Most now see climate change as a serious problem that must be addressed and I surmise that a majority would agree to the proposed upgrade of the energy and transportation infrastructure, especially when the benefits of the growth in employment from a Green New Deal was presented to them. An important element of this presentation should be a demonstration of the current increasing costs resulting from doing nothing. As more citizens feel this in their pocketbooks, this should be easier to prove.

More broadly, there is overwhelming support for a general upgrade to our infrastructure. A 2025 report on American attitudes showed that two-thirds (67%) felt that U.S. infrastructure needed attention and upgrades.[195]

Would American support a carbon tax? Surprisingly, in 2019 a plurality (41%) supported a carbon tax that was not revenue neutral.[196]

---

194 The University of Chicago, Institute for Climate & Sustainable Growth. 2025 Poll: Americans' Views on Climate Change and Policy in 15 Charts. Available at: https://climate.uchicago.edu/news/2025-poll-americans-views-on-climate-change-and-policy-in-15-charts/

195 Accruent. The State of U.S. Infrastructure in 2025—Public Sentiment, Priorities and the Role of Technology. Available at: https://www.accruent.com/resources/blog-posts/state-of-us-infrastructure-2025

196 Michael J. Coren. (2019). Americans: *We need a Carbon Tax, but Keep the Change.* Quartz Daily Brief. Citing a poll by the NORC Center for Public Affairs Research. Available at: https://qz.com/1529997/survey-finds-americans-want-a-carbon-tax/ Also, an article at the Energy Policy Institute of the University of Chicago. Available at: https://epic.uchicago.edu/news/new-poll-nearly-half-of-americans-are-more-convinced-than-they-were-five-years-ago-that-climate-change-is-happening-with-extreme-weather-driving-their-views/

A revenue neutral carbon tax would probably be even more widely supported once people realize that it would financially benefit the large majority of families, while moving the nation as a whole toward renewable energy.

I suggested that universal health care should be a priority. Would American support that? It appears that the answer is yes. In 2024, over six in ten (62%) Americans said that the U.S. Government should ensure that everyone has access to health coverage. A good read about this can be found at the International's Substack.[197]

What about reclaiming the free money now given to large corporations and to the wealthiest portion of our society? The attitudes of citizens about that shows how they react to the prospect of addressing the growing inequality of incomes in American society. The overwhelming majority (79%) support increasing taxes on the rich.[198] Most of the above proposals for addressing rentierism assume attitudes of this kind. None of them would be a particularly hard sell to the American populace, especially if presented without the senseless ideological talk so often mouthed by media pundits.

Although I presented analyses of the need for a living wage, the inadequacy of the current minimum wage and its dire health effects, I did not propose that the federal minimum wage be increased. Would American support such an increase? Again, the answer is yes. The federal minimum wage in 2024 was a laughable $7.25 an hour. Work for an hour and you can buy a cup of coffee! The Raise the Wage Act was passed in 2025. It pushes the minimum wage up very slowly to $17.00 an hour by 2030. Compared to the set rate before this bill, this is good. However, considering the rate of inflation (+2%) as of this writing this is not enough.

There would still be arguments about priority and timelines and a great deal of nitpicking about details in any of these reforms. Universal basic income might be a harder sell but my proposed graduated approach

---

197 International's Substack. Growing Support for Universal Health Coverage: A Shift in American Attitudes. Available at: https://internationaln.substack.com/p/growing-support-for-universal-health

198 Navigator Research. Americans Support Raising Taxes on the Wealthy and Big Corporations. Available at: https://navigatorresearch.org/americans-support-raising-taxes-on-the-wealthy-and-big-corporations/

with tracking and evaluation could be presented as a trial that could be modified or abandoned if there were large negative consequences.

Solutions to Unequal Representation

You may argue about details, but what you cannot challenge is that the current Federal government is currently unlikely to do much of this. That is because in these and many other areas the US Congress, in particular the Senate as currently constituted, does not reflect the views of the majority of US citizens. The Congress should at least roughly reflect the concerns and views of the general population. It does not. At this writing the same is true of the Executive branch of government. The reason for this is not difficult to understand. It is the presence of money provided by a select few to politicians. Yes, politicians need money to get their messages out to the electorate, but the money should come from all citizens, not the tiny group of exceedingly rich people and corporations.

Increasing inequality in income and wealth has been discussed. Here I refer to another kind of inequality that is rampant in the American system: *unequal representation*. A prolific writer explaining and advocating for equality of representation in the US political system is Lawrence Lessig. When I first read one of his earlier books I was struck by it forthrightness in describing how excess money in politics defeats the desires and needs of people on both the right and left.[199] A more recent book, *They Don't Represent Us: Reclaiming Our Democracy*, offers a set of fixes that can be used to address this problem.[200] If they were put in place we might be able to enact some of the reforms I have advocated. His book should be read to appreciate the arguments for and against various proposals.

Political inequality, that is, unequal representation, fosters inequality in incomes and wealth. This relationship exists because most of the latter types of inequality, which have grown so dramatically over the past few decades, arose because of the political process of enacting laws and regulations that shunt money to the wealthy, both individuals and corporations. The laws and regulations as well as enforcement

---

199   Lawrence Lessig. (2012). *Republic, Lost: How Money Corrupts Congress—and a Plan to Stop it*. New York: Hatchette Book Group.

200   Lawrence Lessig. (2019). *They Don't Represent Us: Reclaiming our Democracy*. New York: Dey Street Books.

mechanisms or the lack thereof were put in place or were permitted to remain in place by government representatives, many of whom were elected because of massive direct contributions to their campaigns by groups known as super PACs. In 2024 these groups, which numbered 2,458, spent $2.7 billion during the election cycle.[201]

Focusing on money directly provided to candidates, Lessig suggests an effective reform that would shift raising money to fund campaigns from private to public sources. Funds would be made available to citizens through vouchers or coupons. Every voter would receive $100 in "democracy coupons." They could distribute them to one candidate or to several different ones. This would provide many billions of dollars to candidates. Imagine how this might change the behavior of candidates. Rather than sponsoring $1,500 a plate dinners and cocktail parties for wealthy donors, they would doubtless find it to be more dollar-effective to speak to groups of ordinary citizens in neighborhoods and community gatherings. This process would effectively shift the loyalties of politicians from a small elite group of individuals and families (and corporations) in the upper income tier to all citizens across the income and wealth spectrum. It would bring greater equality to their representation.

Another reform that Lessig advocates to ensure greater equality in representation is enacting federal laws prohibiting gerrymandering. A federal law could be created mandating nonpartisan methods of drawing the boundaries of congressional districts. Congress has the authority to enact such a law. Safe seats achieved through gerrymandering would disappear. More citizens would have a voice in who represents them.

Yet another reform would be to adopt ranked-choice voting. This exists for state-wide elections in Maine and Connecticut. In several other states it is available in some local elections. The are several methods but in general the system permits voters to rank their votes from highest to lowest. Winners can be calculated through ranking rather than through yes-no determinations. For instance, in some systems the candidate with the most number-1 rankings wins but the proportion of his or her 1's must be greater than 50%. Ranked-choice voting promotes greater diversity while ensuring that the rankings of the final winner were the

---

201 Available at Wikipedia: https://en.wikipedia.org/wiki/Super_PAC

highest of the majority of voters. The Wikipedia article on this is good reading.[202]

In two recent presidential elections (2000 and 2016) candidates who lost the popular vote won by obtaining a majority of the Electoral College. This is clearly a problem if you believe in majority rule. A viable solution to this problem (short of a constitutional convention) is the National Popular Vote Interstate Compact. Under this agreement states would select electors who would vote for the winner of the *national* popular vote. As of the end of 2024, states representing 209 electoral votes have entered this agreement. To be effective other state legislatures and governors must enter the compact until the total reaches 270. At that point a president must receive a majority of the popular votes to be elected.[203]

We can move in the direction of greater representation by voting for current candidates that are basing their campaigns on contributions from ordinary citizens and eschewing super PACs. The representatives will be most likely to enact reforms ensuring greater equality of representation. Let us all work together to accomplish this outcome!

If you have reached this point, I thank you dear reader. I hope that the book was not too long-winded and that you have learned things. Thanks again for your interest.

202　Available at: https://en.wikipedia.org/wiki/Ranked-choice_voting_in_the_United_States

203　The official website for the National Popular Vote is: https://www.nationalpopularvote.com/state-status